JAZZ

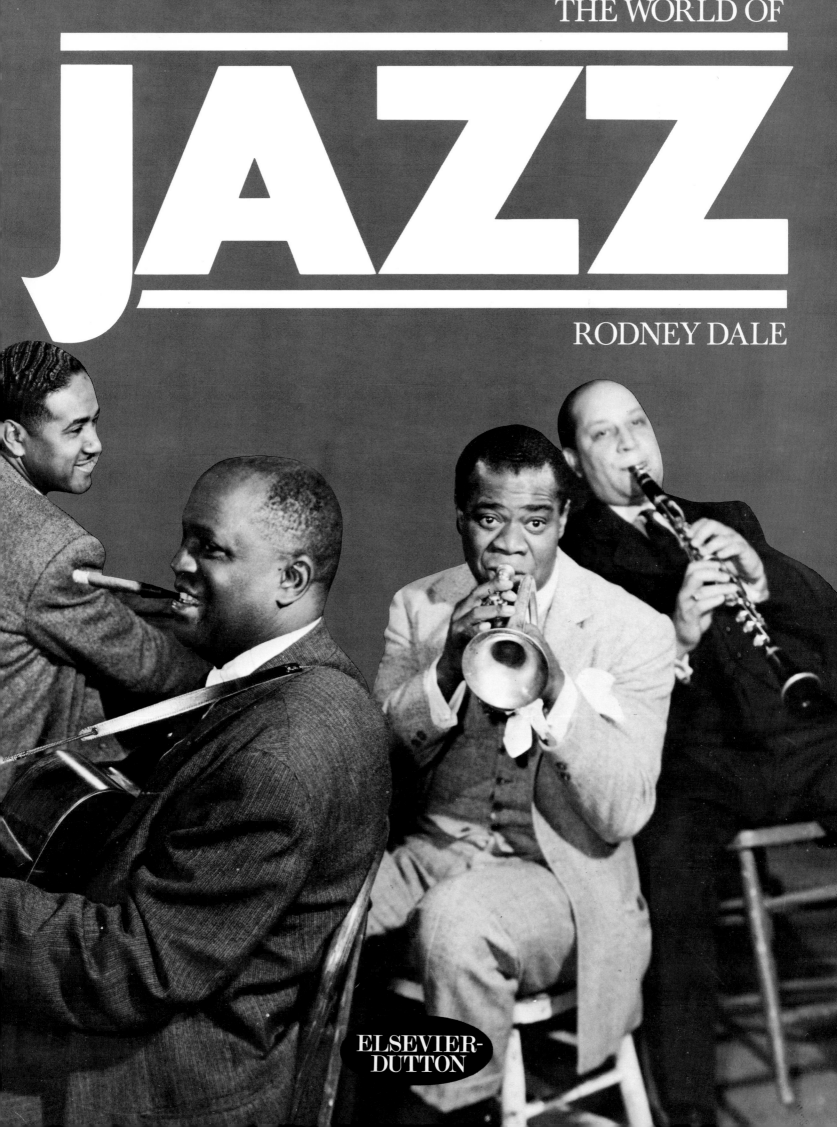

THE WORLD OF
JAZZ

RODNEY DALE

ELSEVIER-
DUTTON

Published in the USA by Elsevier-Dutton
A Division of Sequoia Elsevier Inc

ISBN 0 525 70650 X
Library of Congress
catalog card number: 79-52806

Printed in Hong Kong
by South China Printing Co.

CONTENTS

ACKNOWLEDGEMENTS

I thank my indefatigable picture researcher
Judy Boothroyd, designer Laurence
Bradbury, editor Ann Wilson and typist
Joyce Wrightson – sympathetic production
is a great help to an author, and should not
pass unsung just because it's in the course
of duty.

Turning to picture research, Judy and I
would like to thank the numerous people
who have helped in so many ways; apart
from those acknowledged elsewhere are the
staff of the British Film Institute, Beryl
Bryden, Brian Foskett, Charles Alexander
of The Jazz Centre Society, Nevil
Skrimshire and Matthew Bateson of *Jazz
Journal*, Chris Lakin, and Roy Burchell and
Max Jones of *Melody Maker*.

Finally, when an author thanks his wife
and family 'for their support during his
labours', let it be known that this is no
buzzphrase – it is really what makes it
all possible.

Rodney Dale

INTRODUCTION

Most books on Jazz begin by trying to define Jazz, but even if their definitions are apposite at the time of writing, they may not hold up with the passage of time. Furthermore, there is a fundamental problem in trying to define Jazz in terms of other musical forms. It is like trying to describe colors to the blind: we could describe them in terms of the electromagnetic spectrum, but this would not help much. Perhaps we should simply listen to the music itself, even experiment with it for ourselves, rather than attempt abstract definitions, but some guidelines are necessary.

Jazz is a particular way of playing music, which differs in at least three ways from non-Jazz. First, the player is of far greater importance than he is in non-Jazz: Jazz depends far more on interpretation by individuals than on reproducing a fully annotated score. Following from this is the second element: improvisation – a continual re-interpretation of a given melody or chord sequence (see Appendix 1). However simple this framework, and however strict the rules which govern improvisation, there is still considerable freedom for the player. Third, because of the 'rules' of Jazz, and because there may be more than one musician playing at a time, the rhythms may become very complex – and note that rhythms, internal to the music, must not be confused with beat, which is the fixed timing upon which the rhythms are based.

We must never forget that the world of Jazz is part of the world of music as a whole, to which it is related in many, complex ways. Although we are specifically considering the world of Jazz, we must not forget what is 'outside' it, because it is from outside that the influences which shaped – and are shaping – Jazz come.

But what should we call the music outside the world of Jazz, which above I called non-Jazz? The word 'Classical' is inadmissible, since it has a strict musical meaning. 'Serious' is often used, but this implies that Jazz isn't. The description 'non-Jazz' is neutral enough, provided that we realize that there is no strict frontier between the two worlds. Trying to strictly separate Jazz from non-Jazz can lead to a pointless debate over undefinable terms. It is more helpful to realize that we have to form our own opinions of the demarcation, perhaps with the help of those whose opinions we respect, and that our opinions are liable to change as our experience widens and – most important – as time brings events into perspective.

Consider the world of motoring. This world is concerned with motor cars, but they do not spring into being from nowhere – they are part of a larger world of iron-ore working, glass factories, designers, and so on, which feed materials and labor into a pool which produces motor cars. Now, since motor cars are in general non-political, started their development at about the same time as Jazz did, and were subjected to pressures of development and acceptance as Jazz was, we can carry our comparison a little further. In Britain, enthusiasts classified cars as Veteran (pre-1905), Edwardian (1905–1914) and Vintage (1915–1931), according to their date of manufacture. Enthusiasts suffered from a great snobbishness, averring that any car built after 1931 was worthless. But as time went on, and the patent untruth of this view became clear, the ground was shifted slightly by introducing the category of Post-Vintage Thoroughbred. No one would state categorically that every car made today is a heap of junk, and yet that was a view held by motoring purists thirty years ago – and I know, because I was one of them. We mellow as we age, certainties become doubts, events fall into perspective, and this is as true of Jazz as it is of motor cars. In fact, it is true of all developing art forms. We must be suspect of the need to classify, to hang on to what we 'know' to be good from our own listening; we must work hard to understand the new and the unfamiliar. 'This is old, and therefore good' is countered by the equally invalid 'This is new and therefore better.' 'I know what I like' means 'I like what I know.' We must be sure that we have properly applied ourselves to its study before forming our conclusions.

Motor cars and Jazz, as I said, are in themselves non-political, but the history and experience of Jazz are inseparable from the political and social worlds in which it developed, and this may affect our understanding of the music. For example, if we want to discuss the origins of Jazz, we must talk about slavery and the sufferings of black people. To fully appreciate Jazz, we must understand its background and always approach the music with an open mind.

I/THE JAZZ BACKGROUND

In the past the part which African musical traditions imported into America played in the shaping of Jazz has often been underrated. African music is frequently dismissed as primitive by those whose culture has developed techniques of manufacturing all the instruments of the orchestra and has produced virtuoso performers on those instruments and complex works to be played on them. The fact is that different cultures are just that – different. Comparing and rating them is a task fraught with prejudice and difficulty, and overlooking the finer points of someone else's world from the fastnesses of one's own is all too easy. This may well be one of the reasons for the low esteem in which Jazz was held in its early years, and it is one which we must always try to bear in mind when we are considering the development of the music.

In Africa, rhythm, music and dancing are an integrated part of daily life, whereas in our culture they are put into boxes labelled 'leisure,' 'relaxation,' and so on. We must also bear in mind that African musical traditions are very different from European ones. Rhythmic patterns are far more complex, for African rhythm is not just 'keeping a beat' in our sense, it is an echo of the human voice, even an extension of it.

Similarly, African notions of melody and harmony differ from ours, though they are no less valid, and while the gramophone and radio have done much to make us more receptive to different musical scales and sounds than were our grandparents and their ancestors, it is little wonder that the musical traditions of the African Negro in America were looked upon with, at best, amused tolerance by those unused to them.

In the following sections we will look at the influences in American music toward the end of the last century which played some part, great or small, in shaping Jazz.

The Three Musical Elements

Some people object to music being broken into the three elements of rhythm, melody and harmony, but such an analysis may prove helpful to us here. Certainly, rhythm is fundamental to us, since it is both an element of life itself and the easiest element of music to simulate. The rhythms in life vary, of course. The years, the seasons, night and day, are all familiar but are too slow to be counted as rhythms in a musical sense. On the other hand, the rhythm of the heartbeat and the natural swing of the body and limbs are at musical rates. When we walk, or march, the comfortable pace is determined by the lengths of our limbs, and the same holds good for other bodily rhythms such as clapping or stamping.

Such natural rhythms can be translated into artificial rhythms, for example by banging together any two objects which make a satisfactory sound. The manufacture and playing of percussion instruments, using whatever materials happen to be at hand – from tree-trunks to oil drums – are clearly a logical development.

Music can be enjoyed in two ways: it can be listened to, or it can be participated in. The active, participative enjoyment does not mean that everyone has to play an instrument: members of the audience may use their bodily instruments, such as the hands, feet and voice; or, neither clapping nor singing, they may dance. Such audience participation obviously distinguishes two types of music – compare audience participation at, on the one hand, a recital of Schubert songs, and, on the other, an evening of community singing.

Whatever Jazz is, it certainly has some participative rhythmic element which draws both the mind and the body to it. Although not all music with such an element is Jazz, it may provide a more fruitful area to consider than, for example, that of Mozart's piano concertos or Beethoven's symphonies.

After the fundamental element of rhythm comes melody. It too needs no special equipment. People whistle, sing or hum, gaining, presumably, a certain pleasure from doing so. We can trace the development of instruments capable of producing a melody – the Pan pipes (a set of one-note tubes), the bamboo pipe (a tube with finger holes), animal horns (caused to emit a note by lip vibration) and so on – to the range of brass and woodwind instruments available today. Another route leads from the vibration of a plucked, bowed or struck string to the families of the harp, violin, guitar and piano. Yet another route takes us from tuned percussion instruments to the xylophone, vibraphone, tubular bells, etc. Some would argue that a melody has to be 'tuneful' and that some music lacks this element. At least such music is (generally) not played all on the same note, so that melody is there, even if we are not inspired to sing catchy tunes.

The third element, harmony, is simply a result of singing or playing together. Performance in unison – everyone playing or singing the same note at the same time – is somewhat boring, and the introduction of harmony makes the music more interesting and exciting. It has been suggested that some culturally isolated music-making communities never discovered the art of harmony for themselves, but we cannot test this, and, as Dr Johnson said, 'all reason is against it.' What counts as *acceptable* harmony, however, is a different matter.

The Raw Materials

At this stage I shall use the word 'Jazz' in its loosest sense to indicate many different styles of music, including Blues and Ragtime, which were created by the fusion and development of several kinds of musical tradition. In the pre-Jazz era, there were a number of such raw musical materials, many themselves the product of development and refinement.

One of the strong influences on the emergence of Jazz was the music of popular songs and dances introduced into America by its many immigrants. There were few nations – especially European nations – which did not contribute to this new collective culture, but it was the African Negroes, who had arrived in the country with less willingness than their European colleagues, who did most to found the new art form of Jazz.

Work songs

The raw materials brought to America by the Africans were a particular sense of rhythm and the human voice. Whatever use might have been made of these elements in leisure, they manifested themselves most obviously in work songs – songs sung to accompany labor, in which a leader sings a line and his colleagues respond. Such songs come into their own when they accompany some rhythmic task, such as breaking stone or felling trees. Although there are no contemporary recordings of the earliest work songs (for obvious reasons), the tradition has survived, and there are now recordings which give some idea of what such songs must have sounded like, allowing for the fact that some artificiality is introduced by the mere act of setting out to make a record.

The African Negroes did not, of course, have a monopoly on work songs. Other cultures have discovered the use of song for co-ordinating and lightening tasks – nautical 'Heave-ho' songs are obvious examples.

Gathering of the congregation outside an old downhome church. Church music made a significant contribution to Jazz

Sister Rosetta Tharpe (inset), 1921–73, was trained in the religious musical tradition by her mother, Katie Bell Nubin. She first came to prominence in her late teens in a revue at the Cotton Club in Harlem with Cab Calloway, and continued to appear both with Calloway and with Lucky Millinder before attaining an even greater, worldwide fame as a solo artiste

Ballads

Traditional ballads, another big influence, were brought to America by various cultures, although the way in which they were treated varied. Some would be sung for passive entertainment; others would be adapted for the more active participation of dancing. As time went on, the music was performed not only by local amateurs but by touring professionals who would thus help to spread and intermingle the different styles.

Popular music

Ballads are essentially sung poems, but there is obviously another vast body of popular music which does not come into this category, and which should, at this stage, be considered as a separate raw material.

European and especially Spanish popular music made a particular contribution to Jazz, for such music was subject to the same forces as ballads. At first, popular music was performed locally by those who had brought it with them, but as some of the performers became more professional entertainers, they spread the music over a wider area, and interchanged ideas with others. Soon, there emerged a corpus of entertainment music, a fusion of cultures, culminating in the Minstrel Shows with their vaudeville mixture of songs happy and sad, light and thoughtful, and musical numbers – featuring banjo virtuosi, for example – and other turns. It was the demand for entertainment which both spread what already existed and inspired other performers to come forward and develop the medium.

Church music

America was an ideal land for the evangelical, non-conformist missionaries, and the type of church music they favored was perhaps more abandoned than the conventional hymnal, though it followed the same musical pattern. Again, this was a travelling music and its influence was widespread; it spoke particularly to the slaves, many of whose masters encouraged an active interest in the Christian religion.

The fact that the black participants took the music well beyond its starting point resulted in a new musical expression, Gospel Song. Although Gospel singing incorporated the call-and-response technique of the work song, its development had little to do with the main stream of Jazz, but the form eventually became absorbed into Jazz via more modern developments such as Rhythm and Blues, and Soul, to which we will return.

Brass bands

The music of the brass band is an essential part of army life, of which there was plenty in America, particularly at the time of the Civil War in the first half of the 1860s. Brass bands had two effects: first, they inspired their listeners – everyone loves a marching band; and second, they made available many of the instruments which were later taken up by Jazz musicians.

Apart from their contribution to Jazz, these five raw materials had one factor in common: none of them was confined to a particular locality. True, there would be local performers, each with his own speciality, but no small area was the exclusive home of any one of the five basic forms. They were thus available for all to hear, and for all who were able to practise and develop them. This is important, for it makes the task which now follows of pinpointing the emergence of Jazz more difficult.

2/THE BIRTH OF JAZZ

Canal Street, the main thoroughfare of New Orleans,
about a century ago. In time, it gave its name to
a Blues, as did so many streets in the city

Before looking at the origins of Jazz, we should consider the word itself. Its derivation is obscure. Some attribute it to the French *jaser*, meaning to gossip or chatter; others say that in French the j was pronounced y and that therefore this theory is untenable. Others suggest that it arose from the shout to musicians to 'jazz it,' which begs the question, though it presents the possibility of another French derivation from *jouer*, to play, or *jeux*, games. Jelly Roll Morton said he invented the word in 1902 to distinguish his style from Ragtime, but then, he laid claim to many things, including the invention of Jazz itself, and it does not explain how he chose the word, and why it took so long to gain currency.

Nowadays, there is less reticence in admitting that the word 'jass,' as it was originally spelled, was another of the four-letter ones – which explains any designed obscurity. The pioneers of the music went out of their way to shock as surely as if they had dyed their hair green and spat at the public. The performers adopted strange names, such as Jelly Roll Morton or Speckled Red, and the tunes had strange names – *Potato Head Blues, Pinetop's Boogie Woogie*. Jazz made few concessions. Whether or not it was right to do so, it has won the day.

The date of the word's first attachment to the music will never be known, but it is said to have first appeared in print in the *Chicago Herald* on 1 May 1916. It was then spelled jass; within a year it had changed, via jasz, to Jazz.

Just as the word Blues has many meanings, so does the word Jazz. Originally, it referred to the music we shall discuss in this section, and in some contexts it still does. On the other hand, its wider meaning is that of the title of this book, and includes the styles we shall discuss later.

The Origins

Jazz in its earliest form is generally thought of as having come out of New Orleans at the turn of the century. Although many of the greatest (i.e. remembered) figures of early Jazz were indeed natives of that city, or migrated thither at an early age, there is increasing support for the view that Jazz did not suddenly appear there and nowhere else. However, New Orleans continues to be referred to as 'the cradle of Jazz.'

If, as many suggest, Jazz started as a modified form of brass band music, New Orleans had no monopoly on brass bands. Neither is it reasonable to suppose that this particular invention, unlike any other in the arts or sciences, suddenly arose in one place. As previously stressed, there was much interchange of ideas among performers, and a wide public must have had the opportunity of hearing what was going on in the musical world.

All that can be said with certainty is that Jazz (in the strict sense) is a generally exuberant music which seems to have arisen from a synthesis of the music of the touring minstrel bands and that of the marching bands, with the added influence of other elements of popular music. The New Orleans myth, if we may go so far as to call it that, has arisen from several factors: a 'need' to pinpoint origins, the accidents of birth, and perhaps even an awareness of its potential as a tourist attraction.

It is perhaps also inaccurate to view early Jazz as purely Black music. The influences which led to its flowering are many and varied, and given its geographical spread, some white people may have been involved in its early development, or at least made use of this new form. What is certain is that Jazz was for the working class of the American South.

This brings us to another point to which we will return toward the end of the book – there is now very little parochialism in Jazz; certainly since the last war almost every country has made some contribution to the music. So, although conditions in the Southern States of America at the turn of the century were favorable to the emergence of Jazz it would probably sooner or later have come into being somehow, somewhere. When one listens to a great deal of music of the pre-Jazz age, every now and then one hears Jazz-like snatches, and one cannot help wondering what sounds the great composers may have produced when they were experimenting and improvising. We shall never know, but perhaps Mozart, for example, might have hit on a species of Ragtime which he never wrote down. After all, he did write a waltz with interchangable bars so that the pieces could be assembled in any order with the aid of thrown dice.

Having said all that, it is nevertheless necessary to look to New Orleans as the place where what became Jazz did appear, and at some of the bands and players from that city. According to musicians' memories, the first band to play Jazz – before it was given that name – in New Orleans was that of Charles 'Buddy' Bolden (1868–1931), barber, scandal-sheet editor and cornettist who 'blew his brains out' and spent his life from 1907 in a mental hospital. Bolden appears to have been an organizer as well as a player, who

The Levee and Railway Station, New Orleans, about a hundred years ago. The magnificent paddle steamers were to play an important part in the spread of Jazz, and give livelihood and encouragement to many musicians

would tour the venues of his bands and sit in with them, playing a fine, powerful cornet, doubtless strengthened in the minds of those who heard him – as well as those who did not – by nostalgia.

At the turn of the century, a Bolden line-up comprised cornet, clarinet, trombone, violin, drums, guitar and string bass. In the only known picture of Buddy Bolden's band (pages 20–21), which was taken before 1895, the cornettist is standing behind the guitar player; on his left is the valve trombonist Willie Cornish, and sitting in front of Cornish is clarinettist Frank Lewis. The names of the other musicians are forgotten.

An even rarer piece of Boldeniana than this photograph is a wax cylinder recording of the band – so rare is it, that its existence has never been proved, but it is a delightful legend. In the absence of this vital evidence, what sort of music might we think Bolden played? The presence of the guitar (possibly) and the double bass (certainly) implies that his was not a marching band, and his reported use of a violin, in conjunction with the above, points toward his music being a fusion of minstrel and marching traditions.

Miles Davis – trumpet

The Instruments of Jazz
The term *line-up* refers to the selection of instruments chosen to make a band. Before we look at the composition of bands, let us make a quick survey of the instruments available and their use in Jazz.

Brass
The brass instruments are essentially tubes caused to emit a note by the player pursing his lips against the shaped mouthpiece and blowing a raspberry into it. This act makes the air in the tube vibrate and the air can be persuaded to vibrate in different modes, producing different notes, by the tension of the player's lips. A series of notes can thus be obtained from any suitable tube – animal's horn, conch, bugle, gas-pipe, watering-can and so on. However, only certain notes of the scale are obtainable from such tubes – bugle-calls are the result of making a virtue of necessity – and in order to play the missing notes and produce a complete scale, it is necessary to be able to alter the length of the tube. This may be done either by adding in extra lengths by means of valves (as in the cornet or trumpet), or by providing a slide (as in the slide trombone – though there are valve trombones as well).

Further modifications to the pitch and timbre of the sound may be obtained by the use of trick fingering, lip vibrato, and mutes. Mutes may be designed to plug in to the end of the instrument and give a strangulated sound or manipulated for a 'wah-wah' sound, or they may be makeshift items such as beer mugs, buckets and sink-plungers. Some Jazz brass players from King Oliver onward have been particularly famed for their work with mutes.

The trumpet and cornet differ in shape (the cornet is chunkier) but play in the same range. The flügelhorn is a larger and richer instrument which has more recently come into use in the hands, for example, of Miles Davis. The trombone is well known, as is the tuba, a larger (and therefore deeper-voiced) instrument, and the lowest-pitched of all, the sousaphone. This last, the brass bass, encircles the player; originally the bell appears to have pointed toward the sky, but nowadays is arranged to point forward. All these instruments, with the exception of the slide trombone, have valves.

Dizzy Gillespie – trumpet and *embouchure*

Woody Herman – clarinet

Reeds
Another way of causing the air in a tube to vibrate, and hence produce a note, is to use a mouthpiece with a reed. This is the principle of the clarinet (the first reed instrument of Jazz), the bass clarinet (a less-used, sweet-

Gerry Mulligan – baritone sax

Johnny Hodges – alto sax

Joe Venuti – violin

Ray Brown – string bass

Barney Kessel – guitar

sounding instrument), and the saxophone family (soprano, alto, tenor, baritone and bass). The clarinet and alto sax are straight tubes; all the rest are curved to accommodate their lengths. The note is altered by opening and closing the holes along the tube; since we have but a limited number of fingers and a limited stretch, intricate keywork is provided to enable musical agility. The range is further increased by a hole which, according to whether it is open or shut, determines whether the instrument plays in the high or low register.

As listeners to Jazz will soon realize, the tone of a reed instrument is very much under the control of the player. It is variable according to the material of which the instrument is made, the design of the mouthpiece, the material and set of the reed, and the *embouchure* of the player – the way he sets his mouth to the instrument. When these variations are compared with the latitude acceptable in a non-Jazz player, we at once appreciate an essential quality of Jazz freedom.

The oboe and bassoon have double reeds, which vibrate one against the other. They have been used in Jazz of late, but are not generally thought of as typical Jazz instruments.

Other wind instruments
There are other instruments wherein the air in a tube is caused to vibrate by blowing across it. First there is the piccolo and flute family; since amplification became available the flute has found favor as a Jazz instrument. Second, there are instruments with penny-whistle type mouthpieces, including the recorder family and the Swannee whistle. The last is effectively used as a novelty instrument on occasion.

Stringed instruments
In the stringed instruments, the sound is produced by a vibrating string, amplified by the construction of the body of the instrument, if not by electronic means. The string is caused to vibrate by bowing, plucking, or striking it. Of the orchestral instruments, Jazz uses but the violin and the double bass.

The violin is usually bowed rather than plucked, and is an interesting Jazz instrument in that there are a few very good Jazz violinists. With most other instruments, there are players with a whole range of abilities; the violin seems (fortunately) to be played well or not at all. Foremost exponents of the violin are Stephane Grappelli, Ray Nance, Stuff Smith and Joe Venuti, though some question their status as Jazz musicians.

The double bass, at least in the old days, was usually plucked rather than bowed. In some ways it is one of the Jazz instruments which has advanced most as the music has developed and some very fine bowed playing can now be heard. The double bass is also capable of novelty effects such as slapping, which have their place if not over-used.

The note produced by a string depends on its tension, mass and length. The only quantity which it is convenient to change while playing is length, and the strings can be stopped at desired lengths by pressing them against a fingerboard. The construction of the instrument is such that any note is obtainable within the designed range of the string since it can be stopped anywhere along that range.

This is not the case with the guitar and banjo (ukelele, mandoline, etc.) which have frets on their fingerboards so that the strings are, perforce, stopped at fixed points. Some variation in the note produced may be obtained by pushing the strings sideways thus affecting the tension: in the electric guitar, this may be effected with a lever. The Spanish guitar uses gut or nylon

The only known photograph of cornettist Buddy Bolden and his Orchestra. Bolden stands behind the guitarist; the only others whose names are known are Willie Cornish (valve trombone) and Frank Lewis (clarinet)

strings which produce a more mellow tone than the steel strings more often used on other instruments. The strings are plucked either with the fingers and thumb, or with a plectrum. Both the material of the plectrum, and the position of plucking affect the tone of the instrument. A guitar normally has six strings, but these are sometimes provided in pairs to give a full, rich tone such as is heard from Leadbelly. Another effect is obtained with bottle-neck playing; a ring such as the neck of a bottle is placed on the little finger of the left hand, and a tone similar to that of an Hawaiian guitar is obtained, such as we hear from Muddy Waters.

The construction and playing of the guitar-type instruments differs from those of the violin family in that the former are designed to produce chords of up to as many notes as the instrument has strings. Playing more than one string on the violin or double bass is the exception rather than the rule.

Plucking a steel string gives a very powerful attack to the note produced, and the guitar has benefited greatly from the development of the transistor amplifier which has become better and better at reproducing the note without distortion (though in some cases distortion is the least of anyone's worries).

Muddy Waters – guitarist and Blues singer

The guitar and banjo have always played versatile roles: as solo or band instruments and, if in the band, either as front-line or rhythm section instruments. The guitar accompanying a Blues singer is commonplace, and banjo solos were features of Minstrel Shows. In Jazz bands, the guitar has emerged comparatively recently: amplified, it was first exploited by Charlie Christian who joined Benny Goodman in 1939; sadly, he did not live to benefit from the technique which others so readily took up.

The electric bass guitar is now often used as a substitute for the double bass, compared with which it has both advantages and disadvantages. Its capabilities and techniques are different in that it has frets; it is more portable, though it needs its associated amplifiers and speakers, so this is an advantage only if it is competing with other amplified instruments when this ancillary equipment is needed anyway.

Percussion

Apart from the drum kit, to which we will return in a moment, percussion includes tuned instruments such as the marimba, xylophone, vibraharp – vibes, and the tuned oil drum of the steel band, all of which produce distinctive and sweet sounds. Vibes are the most commonly used in Jazz, and were introduced sparingly in the 1930s by Red Norvo and Lionel Hampton; perhaps the most widely-known exponent is Milt Jackson, late of the Modern Jazz Quartet.

Milt Jackson – vibes

The drummer, like the bassist, has seen a marked change in his role over the last few decades. Originally the drums were there to provide a steady beat, with cross-rhythms according to the skill and taste of the performer. The drummer may have been given a solo in order to demonstrate his art, again according to skill and taste, but he remained firmly in the rhythm section. With the advent of Modern Jazz, however, the drums became more of a front-line instrument, taking part in thoughtful and complex exchanges with other front-line instruments, and opening up new possibilities.

The items in a drum kit are many, and vary according to the style of the player. Staple diet is the bass drum operated with a pedal, the hi-hat cymbal operated with another pedal, and the snare drum (a wire snare vibrates against its lower skin), all borrowed from marching band practice. There can also be a selection of other cymbals, sometimes with rivets round the edges to give a distinctive ring, tom-toms, wood blocks, cow bells and skulls. The last three may have been introduced to obviate the shortcomings of pre-electric

The Count Basie Orchestra

recording, and may be eschewed by modern drummers.

Although the principle of drumming is obvious, the role of the drummer is crucial, and far more difficult than appears at first sight. Nothing can upset a band more than a tasteless drummer.

Max Roach – drums

Keyboards

Our final selection is from instruments played with keyboards, of which the most important during the emergence of Jazz was the piano. Today, keyboards embraces the conventional piano, the organ, electric piano, and other electronic marvels.

The pianist is the only musician who does not carry his instrument about with him, bearing the derisive cries of his fellows stoically, never knowing what instrument the organizers are going to provide for him to play – if, indeed, they remember to provide an instrument at all.

The piano has always been an ambiguous instrument, sometimes part of the rhythm section, sometimes part of the front line. Apart from the guitar, the piano is one of the few instruments capable of being played solo for any length of time without becoming wearisome, and certainly the only one which can produce ten – or even more – notes at a time. On the other hand, its notes are immutably fixed by the construction and tuning of the instrument and in that respect it is more limited than any other.

The use of the harmonium or organ in Jazz has generally been more of a novelty than an advance in the art. More recently, the electronic keyboard instruments have come into their own and introduced the possibility of effects to be exploited both in Jazz and in other popular music.

This brief survey purports to be neither complete historically, nor an instruction manual for would-be players. My purpose has been to explain some of the capabilities and limitations of the instruments used in Jazz which may help the listener to understand why the music sounds as it does.

Thelonious Monk – piano

The Jazz Band

Many people who want to make music choose a particular instrument because it happens to be handy. This certainly happened in the early days of Jazz, and one theory is that the American armies had left behind piles of instruments of the types found in military bands – trumpets, cornets, trombones, clarinets – which were thus readily available to aspiring musicians.

We have already used the term *front-line* instruments, and its meaning is almost self-explanatory – those instruments which stand at the front of the band and play the melody and its accompaniment. That the discarded instruments were the makings of front lines is of course no accident, for a marching band would naturally want to use instruments with complementary *voices*, and avoid the problems – both numerical and postural – of introducing a violin section, for instance.

To complement the front line, a *rhythm section*, to which we have also referred above, is needed. Its instrumentalists were commonly a drummer, combining the work of several marching men, a string or brass bass, guitar or banjo, and perhaps a piano. With the exception of the brass bass, these are all minstrel or spasm band instruments. Thus the usual line up of a Jazz band has its origins both in the marching bands and in the minstrel and spasm bands, to which we will turn shortly.

We now have the outline of what might be called a conventional Jazz band of some six or seven players, the reasons for its line up being both accidental, because of the availability of the instruments, and practical, because of the

complementary nature of their voices. The role of the trumpet (or cornet) – that of playing the melody while the trombone and clarinet provide the lower and higher voices – is clearly crucial, so more often than not the trumpeter (or cornettist) was (and is) the leader of the band.

As time went on and Jazz became an established art form, many other instruments, as we saw above, were pressed into service, though some are more suited to the medium than others. There is one particular instrument, however, which should be mentioned here as an essential part of Jazz, though it did not arrive on the scene until later – the saxophone.

The saxophone family was developed by Adolphe Sax, who settled in Paris in the 1840s; his French patent was taken out in 1846. The instrument found some work in military bands, but was little used outside France until the end of the last century. It somehow became associated with Jazz in about 1915, and since then has become more identified with Jazz than any other instrument. The reason probably lies in the tone of the saxophone; according to the competence of the player, it is capable of a wide range of expression, and its similarity to the human voice makes it sympathetic to the spirit of the music. Adam Carse wrote in 1939: 'When it became popular as a dance-band instrument the saxophone lost status and dignity, and a style of playing developed which was mercifully never known to the originator.' However, I would venture to suggest that Adolphe Sax, since he saw fit to design an instrument which sounded like that, would be delighted by the virtuosi of today, and at the pleasure which his invention has given to so many people.

A Spasm Band – an impromptu gathering for maximum enjoyment – sometimes called a Jug Band because of the strong bass notes produced by the player with the jug

Spasm Bands

It is one thing to acquire ready-made instruments; another to make them yourself. Spasm bands were groups of musicians who made and played their own instruments, and an oft-cited early example is Stale Bread Charlie's Spasm Band which toured with Doc Malney's Minstrel Show in the 1890s.

Home-made instruments include guitars, banjos and fiddles made from wooden boxes; comb-and-paper or its improved version, the kazoo; kettles and lengths of pipe played with a trumpet *embouchure*; large cans and jugs into which raspberries are blown to give fine bass notes; tea-chest string bass; and an assortment of bells, whistles and percussion instruments, including kitchen utensils, suitcases and the washboard played with thimbles or brush heads.

Spasm bands were important as they encouraged the making of music, however primitive, and it was with such a band that Edward 'Kid' Ory earned the money to buy his first trombone. In the 1920s, such masters as Johnny Dodds played with spasm bands, or skiffle groups as they came to be called, in Chicago, showing that an extremely enjoyable and exciting noise can be made without the use of conventional instruments. The 1950s saw a skiffle revival which again probably did more good than harm in encouraging aspiring young musicians.

One can therefore sum up by saying that Jazz, New Orleans Jazz as we think of it, owes its origin to the constraints of Western instruments, with their generally fixed scales; and to the musical tradition of the marching band modified by shifting the accentuated beats, making it ragged, ragging it. Since it emerged at about the same time as piano Ragtime, there was clearly a need for a new descriptive word to distinguish it. The need was perceived by Jelly Roll Morton, even if he did not invent the word.

Riverboats and Migration

Although we have placed Jazz in New Orleans, we have intimated that it may well have begun to emerge elsewhere at about the same time – that the climate was right for it. Certainly it was not static, for there were ready-made channels for its dissemination – the vaudeville circuits. There were vaudeville bands with line-ups and opportunities for playing Jazz.

There was thus a diffusion of talent about the country, but two factors were especially important: the railroad and the Mississippi River. The first is self-explanatory – it is a method of travelling from A to B comparatively swiftly. But the second needs further consideration, for the riverboats were more than a means of transport.

The Mississippi is one of the world's largest rivers and the most important in North America. Since it is over 4000 miles long, yet falls less than one-third of a mile in that length, it is slow flowing and comparatively wide. From the last century, great paddle-steamers plied the river; for commerce, passenger transport – and pleasure. If you're going to move a few hundred tons of cargo, why not add a suitable superstructure and move a few hundred passengers as well, entertaining them as you go? So it was that the show-boats often carried a Jazz band, and many of the best musicians out of New Orleans spent some time during their careers in such bands, before leaving the boat at one of the up-river cities, particularly St Louis, Kansas City (on the Missouri) or Davenport, on the way to Chicago. Nor was the enjoyment of the music of the bands confined to the passengers on the boats: on a pleasure trip it was customary for them to stop en route so that the land-bound could enjoy them as well. Thus the riverboats both spread the word and inspiration of Jazz, and acted partly as nurseries, partly as free transport

A street band in present-day New Orleans

Paulie Freed and his Rhythmicians in the Gennett
recording studios

to the musicians who migrated northward from the second decade of the century onward.

Captain Joseph Streckfus owned a number of Mississippi riverboats and was – perhaps unwittingly – responsible for the development of many musicians (not to mention their translation from New Orleans to points up river), via his talent-spotting bandleaders. Foremost among these were the trumpeter Charlie Creath (1890–1951) and the pianist Fate Marable (1890–1947), both of whom spent most of their working lives on the riverboats. Neither Creath's nor Marable's band seems to have recorded at any stage, so we can only infer their quality from their long tenures and their top line-ups.

Chicago

With the Mississippi route open, Chicago became the great center for Jazz for a number of reasons. It was – and is – a very much larger city than New Orleans, with a proportionately greater Black population toward which, in the 1910s, it had a somewhat less oppressive attitude than areas further south. The closing of the New Orleans red light district, Storyville, in 1917 is often said to have caused the exodus, but there is plenty of evidence to show that Chicago was becoming an attractive center before that event. Nor was the move the result of a random migration which just happened to end there. The city had places of entertainment of all types, with what would today be

A paddle steamer of the Streckfus line – note the initials J.S. on the paddle cover

called talent scouts always on the look-out for new attractions – and what better than Jazz bands?

The Jazz scene then was therefore much as it is today: promoters providing venues, musicians becoming band leaders and inviting others to join them, a constant traffic of musicians between one band and another, and tours of gigs (one-night stands), seasons as resident bands, and recording sessions.

The recording sessions are particularly important, because the recording industry centered on Chicago, and though it was not until about 1920 that it came into its own as a producer of a new consumer product – the phonograph and the records to go with it – when it did catch on it did so like wildfire. Mamie Smith's 1920 recording of *Crazy Blues* sold over a million pressings in its first six months, and from then on there was a constant stream of musicians – known and unknown – seeking similar success. This is brought out by the exchange, quoted on the right, between the pianist Pinetop Smith and his friend Mr X at the start of Pinetop's record *Jump Steady Blues* (1929).

There were other ways of making money playing on these here records. The ebullient pianist Will Ezell, for example, was wont to claim travelling expenses from Texas, but it was suspected that he lived just round the corner from the studios.

However, Jazz cannot be considered *in vacuo,* and there were other reasons for the migration north in the second decade of the century. It must not be forgotten that in the years 1914–18 there was a 'war to end all wars' being waged in Europe, and that Thomas Woodrow Wilson, 28th President of the USA, declared war on Germany in April 1917 in order to 'make the world safe for democracy.' The preparation for and participation in this activity created a large number of jobs in certain centers, thus playing a significant part in the migration from South to North. So although we may get the impression that Jazz was confined mainly to New Orleans (whence it sprang) and Chicago (where the recording studios were) and points between, musicians were entertaining audiences across the country from Los Angeles in the West to New York City in the East.

Mr X: Why, hello there Pinetop, what are you doin sittin roun here looking so sad with your head hung down?

Pinetop: I jes thinkin bout all these piano players goin roun here makin big money playin on these here records

Mr X: Why don't *you* play on some of these records?

Pinetop: Boy, that's a good idea, I b'lieve I start rehearsin right now.

Pinetop then plays his very beautiful Boogie, and at the end:

Pinetop: Well, how's that?

Mr X: Oh boy, that ought to get it.

The Pioneers of Jazz

For information on the pioneers of Jazz, we have, until the advent of recording, to rely on the memories of musicians. Who did what, where and when, and how well they did it, is often a matter of conjecture. It was generally many years after the events that the social historians of Jazz came on the scene, and the survivors of the early days to whom they talked tended to make extravagant claims on behalf of both themselves and others; these memories were then accepted or modified according to the preconceptions and biases of the interviewers, and set down in print, thus giving them an often unwarranted seal of accuracy.

It was almost a quarter of a century after the emergence of Jazz that phonograph records of the music were made, and only from that point do we have the means to judge it for ouselves. However, from recordings and reminiscences we can form some opinion about which musicians made a significant contribution to the shaping of Jazz, and in the pages that follow we look at the careers of some of the men who came out of New Orleans, and who were born before or around the turn of the century. Their inclusion here is not to acknowledge them all as equally great, and no one would agree even if there was an attempt to grade them. Their intertwining careers give rise to some repetition, but this helps to build a general picture of the bands through which the music took shape, and to introduce other characters, each of whom made some contribution.

LOUIS ARMSTRONG

Fittingly, the first name in our list is Louis Armstrong who is, to many people, the personification of Jazz – and not without reason. He was born in New Orleans, probably on Independence Day 1900. He spent an impoverished childhood surrounded by the music of New Orleans and earned a little money himself by singing in the streets: how his childhood voice might have compared with the distinctive tones of his later years is worth a few moments' reflection.

On the eve of the New Year 1913 he fired a jubilant pistol shot in the street, was arrested and sent to the Waifs' Home. It was here that he learned to play the cornet, inspired by his tutor in the home, Peter Davis. After he was released, Louis played for various bands and during this time he met King Oliver who was, in spite of the many who would bask in Louis's reflected glory by claiming to have taught him Jazz, the one who actually did.

We tend to think of musicians only in terms of their music but comparatively few were able to make a permanent living by their playing alone and Louis was no exception at this stage. So while he was making music in other people's leisure hours, he was also working hard during the day selling coal.

Oliver moved to Chicago in 1918, saying that one day he hoped to be able to send for Louis. Louis stayed in New Orleans, and took Oliver's place in Kid Ory's Band, working the riverboats, and playing in street parades. In 1922 Oliver, who was playing at Chicago's Lincoln Gardens, invited Armstrong to join him as second cornet. It is often suggested that Oliver was working on the principle 'if you can't beat 'em, join 'em,' but this must be somewhat unsound since America is a large country and Armstrong seems to have had no urge to leave New Orleans except at Oliver's summons.

After a couple of years with Oliver, during which time he made his first recordings (notable not least for their capturing of the fabulous two-cornet breaks), Armstrong left to tour with Fletcher Henderson, with whom he also played a six-month residency at the Roseland Ballroom, New York. In the autumn of 1925, he left Henderson and joined his second wife, Lil Hardin Armstrong, and her Dreamland Syncopators in Chicago. On 12 November he made the first of the Hot 5 recordings, one of the never-to-be-surpassed feats of Jazz of that period.

During the next few years, Armstrong

The personification of Jazz – Louis Armstrong

Zutty Singleton, one of the foremost traditional drummers from New Orleans

The New Orleans Seven – Zutty Singleton (dms), Red Callender (bass), Kid Ory (tmb), Charlie Beale (pno), Bud Scott (bjo), Louis Armstrong (tpt), Barney Bigard (clt)

Louis Armstrong – on and off duty on a UK tour

played with many of the top bands – Carroll Dickerson, Clarence Jones, Luis Russell, Erskine Tate. He also made countless records, for instance accompanying Blues singers such as Bessie Smith. At the beginning of the 1930s he moved from Jazz and Blues toward popular ballads; he sang and clowned; he appeared on stage and film set; and he became what would nowadays be called 'a personality.'

It is of note that Armstrong, with his sympathetic pianist Earl Hines and drummer Zutty Singleton, attempted to run a night club in Chicago for a short period. But the venture was unsuccessful; Armstrong was no businessman, neither was he a natural leader – his name was made through entertainment, not from gathering talent.

He visited Europe for the first time in 1932, and again for an extended tour in 1933–35, continuing as a showman, one of the greatest-ever ambassadors of Jazz. He continued to tour the States extensively until after the war, and in 1947 formed the first of the Louis Armstrong All Stars groups. He now started to travel all over the world, visiting London again in 1956; there must be few major countries he did not play in. In the last few years his health was not always good, though this is hardly surprising in one who led such a strenuous life.

He made many film appearances, but that when he sang *Hello, Dolly* in the film of that name (1969) is particularly noteworthy in that, although he sang for less than one minute, thousands of people went to see the film just to savor that minute.

Louis continued to play until he suffered a heart attack in March 1971. He died two days after his 72nd birthday, mourned as one of the greatest Jazz musicians of all time.

BABY DODDS

Called 'Baby' Dodds to distinguish him from his elder brother Johnny, this drummer was doubtless the greatest to emerge from New Orleans, where he was born in 1898. He worked in that city, and on the riverboats with Fate Marable, until he joined his brother in King Oliver's Band in Chicago in 1921. He stayed with Oliver for three years, and was then attached to a number of bands, notably Freddie Keppard's, until 1928, when he joined his brother and Natty Dominique for two years at Kelly's Stable, Chicago.

He continued to play and record with many of his brother's groups until Johnny's death; he also assisted another brother, Bill, in the cab business in the 1930s. Baby Dodds was part of the New Orleans Revival of the 1940s, but a number of strokes curtailed his playing from 1949, and although he continued to perform when he could, he had to retire completely in 1957. He died in 1959.

JOHNNY DODDS

Johnny Dodds, born in New Orleans in 1892, taught himself to play the clarinet, and in 1911 he joined Kid Ory's Band with which he stayed until the end of the decade. He then went on tour, revisited New Orleans for a short period and then moved to Chicago, which he made his home for the rest of his life. In Chicago, he was a key member of

Warren 'Baby' Dodds

Natty Dominique

Johnny Dodds

King Oliver's Creole Jazz Band, being joined by his brother, Baby Dodds, on drums and, of course, Louis Armstrong. In the latter half of the 1920s, Johnny Dodds made a large number of recordings with many groups: classics of his style. The most important were those with the Hot 5, mentioned below, and with Jelly Roll Morton.

Dodds became less well known in the 1930s – during the Depression he joined his brothers in the cab business – but later he returned to music and made some recordings in the last two years of his life before suffering a series of strokes. He died in 1940 at the age of 47, just before the New Orleans Revival in which he would have undoubtedly been a key figure had he lived. To many, Dodds's tone and fluency is the quintessence of New Orleans clarinet playing.

HOT 5

There is no doubt that one of Louis Armstrong's most important musical achievements was assembling his Hot 5 in 1925–27, solely for the purpose of recording. The lasting popularity of these recordings has no doubt surpassed anyone's wildest dreams.

Armstrong, on cornet in the earlier sessions, and on trumpet in the later ones, was in his prime. In combination with clarinettist Johnny Dodds and trombonist Kid Ory, the whole was certainly greater than the sum of its considerable parts. King Oliver's Band had specialized in collective improvisation: the Hot 5, with three individualists in its front line, concentrated on solos and offered a refinement of New Orleans Jazz which it is difficult to better.

Part of the lightness lies in the small rhythm section – the banjo of Johnny St Cyr, and the piano of Lil Hardin, by that time Armstrong's second wife. Although St Cyr was one of the best banjo players to come out of New Orleans, Lil Hardin was by no means the world's best pianist – but at least she knew what was wanted.

In May 1927, the Hot 5 became the Hot 7 for one week with the addition of the tuba of Pete Briggs and the drums of Baby Dodds, Johnny's brother.

JOHNNY St CYR

The banjoist Johnny St Cyr was born in New Orleans (La) in 1890; his father played flute and guitar and Johnny learned the guitar and banjo. His musical path crossed those of his fellows in the Hot 5; he played in Kid Ory's Band in 1914–16, on the riverboats, and with King Oliver in Chicago.

Johnny St Cyr

The Hot 5 – Louis Armstrong (tpt), Johnny St Cyr (bjo), Johnny Dodds (clt), Kid Ory (tmb), Lil Hardin Armstrong (pno)

To Kid Muggsy from Louis Armstrong

He made his name with the Hot 5 and Red Hot Peppers recordings in the 1920s, but he then became inactive. For some reason the start of the New Orleans Revival seems to have passed him by. It was not until later that he returned to the Jazz scene, and the first and finest Jazz banjo-player was rediscovered. He died in 1966.

KID ORY

Kid Ory was born in La Place (La) on Christmas Day 1886. He is chiefly, and rightly, remembered as a pioneer of the 'tailgate' trombone – a style said to have been named after the custom of placing the trombonist at the back of a band waggon with his slide protruding over the lowered tailgate – though why this positioning should cause the trombonist to play *glissandi* is not stated. However, Ory was able to play many other instruments and, an early entrepreneur, he organized a five-piece spasm band which earned him enough to buy his first trombone. His New Orleans bands featured at one time or another the brass of Louis Armstrong, Papa Mutt Carey and King Oliver, and the reeds of Sidney Bechet, Johnny Dodds, George Lewis and Jimmie Noone.

Ory studied and worked in Los Angeles from 1919 to 1924 and then moved to

Edward 'Kid' Ory

Kid Ory's Original Creole Jazz Band in the early 1920s in California – indicative of the spread of Jazz

King Oliver's Creole Jazz Band – Johnny Dodds (clt), Baby Dodds (dms), Honoré Dutrey (tmb), Louis Armstrong (2nd cnt), King Oliver (cnt & ldr),

Lil Hardin (pno), Bill Johnson (bjo/bass)

Chicago, where he played with many of the top bands, and made some of his most famous recordings with the Hot 5, the Hot 7 and the Red Hot Peppers. In 1930 he returned to Los Angeles, played a little, then retired from music to help his brother on a chicken farm. At the beginning of the 1940s he returned to music, first with Barney Bigard, then with Bunk Johnson, and found himself part of the new interest in old Jazz. Ill health forced him into retirement again in the mid-1950s, but he continued to play and tour when he was able. He died in Hawaii in 1973.

KING OLIVER

The illustrious name of King Oliver has appeared many times already. Joe Oliver was born somewhere in Louisiana in 1885; he moved to New Orleans as a boy, and studied first the trombone and then the cornet, which remained his instrument thereafter. He played in several New Orleans bands, and led his own, until he moved to Chicago in 1918. Before the move he played in Kid Ory's Band, and it was Ory who named him 'King.'

In Chicago, he played with both Lawrence Duhé and Bill Johnson, eventually taking over the former's band which emerged as King Oliver's Creole Jazz Band and which held a legendary position in the World of Jazz until 1924. This was the band which included Louis Armstrong and Johnny Dodds. Indeed, many of the best Jazz musicians of the day played for or with Oliver at one time or another.

In its time, King Oliver's Creole Jazz Band produced a sound of collective improvisation which has never been bettered and, being the first Black band to record (1923) that sound is enshrined for ever. The very quintessence of New Orleans music is here – the two cornets (Oliver and Armstrong) playing the melody, with Oliver's unique use of mutes; the lower voice filled with Honoré Dutrey's trombone; Dodds's clarinet fluently filling the higher voice of the band. The emphasis was on the collective sound, as it is in a marching band: solos were not a feature of earlier Jazz. The real excitement is to be found in the Oliver-Armstrong two-cornet breaks, different every time. Their secret lay in the very close mental rapport between the two men; it is said that Oliver would quietly sing his next idea into Louis's ear so that the harmony was there when the time came for the execution.

The Creole Jazz Band rhythm section comprised Bud Scott, an equal of Johnny St Cyr on banjo, Lil Hardin, and Baby Dodds.

Jimmie Noone

After his Creole Jazz Band broke up, Oliver formed his Dixie Syncopators which flourished and recorded for two years. In 1928 he moved to New York, but it was the end of his years of genius: a brass player needs a good *embouchure*, and Oliver suffered much from dental problems. He retired from music, settled in Savannah (Ga) and died in obscurity before reaching the age of 53, in 1938.

FREDDIE KEPPARD

King Oliver's was the first Negro band to record, but the honor could have fallen to Freddie Keppard in 1916 had that trumpeter not feared that to record was to lay his music open to copying, a fear to some extent akin to the belief that the camera steals part of the subject's soul. No doubt gramophone records have taught aspiring musicians, from Charlie Parker downward, a great deal, but they have also created audiences eager to hear the real thing, and provided enormous royalties for the luckier performers. Unfortunately, by the time Keppard did decide to record, he was past it and we shall never know what he sounded like in his prime.

Keppard was born in New Orleans in 1889 and his early career followed much the same pattern as King Oliver's: brass bands in his native city and a move to Chicago. He and Oliver were the two most influential New Orleans horn players during the emergence of Jazz. He spent the 1920s in Chicago, playing with many of the well-known bands, including Doc Cook(e)'s Dreamland Orchestra, and Erskine Tate's Vendome Orchestra. He died in 1933 after some years of failing health.

JIMMIE NOONE

Of the New Orleans clarinettists who lived to record, Noone was one of the greatest. He was born near New Orleans in 1895, moved there in his boyhood, and learned to play guitar and clarinet. He studied the latter with Sidney Bechet, whom he replaced in Freddie Keppard's band in about 1910. He went on to play with many other great musicians – Papa Celestin, Kid Ory and Buddy Petit – and formed the Young Olympia Band with the last. Toward the end of the decade he moved to Chicago and played with Doc Cook's Dreamland Orchestra for much of the time, though he also played and recorded with King Oliver and Tommy Ladnier.

In 1926 he formed his own group at Chicago's Apex Club, notable also for the presence of pianist Earl Hines. He continued to lead bands, mainly in Chicago, and to record effectively from time to time. He never retired from Jazz, though his popularity was eclipsed by the rise of Swing – ironically, since he had been the inspiration of Benny Goodman. However, he returned to popularity at the beginning of the 1940s, but died of a heart attack a few days before his 50th birthday, in 1944.

JELLY ROLL MORTON

In a brief survey of those who were part of New Orleans Jazz in its formation, whom should we leave out? There are of course dozens of names that could be included, given space, and some not in the text appear in the pictures – if a picture speaks a thousand words, they are doing well. However, who would argue about the inclusion of Jelly Roll Morton as one of the few who contributed uniquely to Jazz? One or two, I know, but the majority recognize his genius, as well as the extravagance of his claims and imagination, which antagonized many during his life.

Morton was born in Gulfport (La) in 1885 and had some musical training, first on the guitar and later the piano. At the beginning of the century he found his way to Storyville, the center of New Orleans prostitution brought into being by Alderman Story in 1897. There was always a demand for 'professors' at the piano in Storyville sporting-houses, and Morton was one of the best. He started with the Ragtime style (see Chapter 4) and developed it by bringing to it all that his capacious musical memory stored. He played rhythms so subtle that some derogatory critics said that he had no sense of timing.

Although he was able to play with a charming simplicity, Morton believed that the piano should, when played as a solo instrument, be able to emulate a whole band, and a comparison of his solo compositions with the same played by his Red Hot Peppers (1926–30) shows his belief being put, incredibly, into practice.

The latter half of the 1920s was Morton's heyday, and he behaved larger than life – spending money whenever he had it, and taking more interest in gambling than in music. His popularity declined in the 1930s but he was finally found in Washington (DC) by Alan Lomax and persuaded (not, one imagines, a difficult task), to place the story of his life and his reminiscences on record for the Library of Congress Archive (1938). Taken with appropriate salt, these recordings give an interesting insight into the world of Jazz seen through Morton's eyes. He moved to California in 1940, became ill and died the following year.

Though Morton produced a markedly individual piano sound, composed Jazz of a type that has never been bettered, and played with many of the leading musicians of his time, it is difficult to show that he directly influenced any particular school of music. What he did do was to point to the crucial role of the composer/arranger in Jazz: he understood the music, he understood the instruments, and he wrote for the musicians he chose to play with him.

Reading his story again, some 25 years wiser than when I first came across it, I am convinced that his was a schizoid personality, which goes a long way to explaining his life and illusions, and possibly why he was able to take his music to the peak of one of the mountains in the range, and leave it there.

Tommy Ladnier

Jelly Roll Morton and his Red Hot Peppers – Andrew Hilaire (dms), Kid Ory (tmb), George Mitchell (tpt), John Lindsay (bass), Jelly Roll Morton (pno),

Johnny St Cyr (bjo), Omer Simeon (clt) – the pinnacle of recorded, arranged, New Orleans Jazz

Although we think of the Blues as an essential part of the world of Jazz, which nowadays it is, it is important to separate it from the Jazz at the turn of the century discussed in the previous chapter.

We have already seen that the work song was a rhythmic chant to accompany labor, with a leader evoking responses from his colleagues. If we look at the form further, we find it was often used for passing messages among the workers, or for just telling a story. The first example on the right is taken from a work song; the second is a more developed, sophisticated version which could well have started its life in the same way. The tradition of music as an integral part of life is clearly carried through here, and owes little to any influence other than the African. It was from this type of music that the Blues was developed, rather than from the combination of musical styles limited by the constraints of Western tradition which produced New Orleans Jazz. The early Blues is quite separate from that stream.

If we are at all familiar with the form, we think of the Blues as dealing with basic inevitabilities – life and death, eating and sleeping, loving and losing – in the form of a poem, usually with 12-bar stanzas of three lines each, of which the second is a modified form of the first, as in the examples on the right.

In print it looks banal – where is the meter and the rhyme? The Blues has to be sung to take on its poetry and beauty and feeling and rhythm and rhyme, and no description on paper is a substitute for its performance, for it is (in its emergence, at any rate) a traditional music, handed down by singers who could neither read nor write words, let alone musical notation – which in any case is unable to cope adequately with the music.

Here we find one of the differences between the Blues and New Orleans Jazz: it is not just that we find it difficult to notate the rhythmic complexity. Blues has a musical scale of its own – the so-called 'blue notes' do not fit properly into our Western scales, which are themselves fixed by the struc-

Leader: Did you hear about that water boy getting drownded
Response: In Mobile Bay?

L: It was one Sunday morning
R: Lawd, Lawd, Lawd
   The preacher went a-huntin'
      Lawd, Lawd, Lawd
   He carried 'long his shotgun
      Lawd, Lawd, Lawd
         etc.

2.19 train done took my baby away
2.19 train took my bab'way
2.17 bring her back some day

Or:

I walked all night long with my 32–20 in my hand
Walked all night, 32–20 in my hand
Looking for my woman, well she's gone off with another man.

Blues titles and lyrics show a frequent preoccupation with railroad imagery and the music reflects the pounding rhythms of the trains

tures of our musical instruments. Although the human voice can manage these notes, most instruments can not, with the inevitable debasing results. The debasement is exacerbated by the fact that the blue notes are *approximated* by flattening the third and the seventh in the scale, so that now there are few performers who know the difference.

This state of affairs would have been different had there been a fixed-note instrument with a Blues scale, but nobody seems to have thought of making one – unlike, for example, the Scots, who have preserved their own pentatonic scale on the bagpipes. The need for a special Blues instrument may have been obviated by the existence of the guitar, since it is possible to play in-between notes on it by manipulating the strings. The guitar was, and is, often used by Blues singers to accompany themselves, and not solely because it is portable. Its ability to play blue notes is as important as the complement it offers to the human voice. The quality of Blues accompaniment is to be judged by the interplay of the voice and instrumental answering phrase – see below.

It should be mentioned that, although we think of the Blues as a 12-bar form (the meaning of which is explained in Appendix 1), it is thought that the very early Blues, emerging perhaps a century ago, may have been of an 8-bar form (first line not repeated), which would then lead to a 16-bar form (two couplets).

The rationale behind the repeated first line of the 12-bar Blues is said to be that it gives the singer-composer time to devise his final line while he is singing the repeat, but that may be an over-simplification.

In listening to Blues – essential, since no amount of description will do the form justice – it will be noticed that the words of each line do not fill the whole 4-bar musical accompaniment. Most of the last 2 bars of each 4-bar section are filled by the accompanist(s), who frames some appropriate

A railroad section gang, one of the cradles of work songs

Ma Rainey and her Wildcat Jazz Band, 1923 –
Gabriel Washington (dms), Al Wynn (tmb), Dave
Nelson (tpt), Ma Rainey (sgr & ldr), Eddie Pollack
(sax), Thomas A Dorsey (pno)

musical answer to the singer's phrasing, which can be very beautiful. Although such integration is a later development, it clearly makes for a very tidy, not to say delicate, form. It may therefore be the development of the form which decided the repeat of the line, rather than vice versa.

Definitions

Nowadays, the title 'Blues' may be applied to many different forms of music. So far, I have been referring particularly to the Archaic Blues, which to some extent may have to be imagined, since time and commercialism have had their effects. The mere act of recording, as we have remarked, introduces artificiality. The other senses in which the word 'Blues' may be used are what might be classified as Rural, Urban and General.

Rural Blues is as much of the Archaic Blues as can remain when its performers have had the opportunity of listening to one another, exchanging ideas, and entering recording studios.

Urban Blues is a developed form, which might alternatively be termed Vaudeville Blues. It does not necessarily adhere to the 12-bar form and has words and a style of performance markedly different from those of the Rural Blues.

Sometimes the word Blues is used indiscriminately for the title of any number played slowly, or even fast; thus is the currency debased. It may be even further debased by those who use the term to describe certain kinds of popular music which may have no direct connection with Blues or even Jazz.

Blues Singers

One of the essential instruments of the Blues is the human voice. There are many who have sung Blues of all types, and whom we will meet in the following pages. Generally, the male singers are instrumentalists and the females are not. This is not just an extension of the fact that there are comparatively few female instrumentalists; it has always been an added artistic attraction to have a girl singer with a band, and there is a difference in quality between male and female voices.

Thus we find that our male singers accompanied themselves, almost always on the guitar, and sang – at least in their earlier days – a more Rural Blues; our female singers were artistes in their own right and turned the Rural Blues into Vaudeville Blues almost from the start.

It was here that the influence of technology on Jazz (see Appendix 2) made itself felt once again, through the medium of the phonograph. As long as there is something to sell to the public, manufacturers will find new ways of exploiting it, and in the early 1920s the idea of the Race Record was born – a polite way of saying records of Negro performers aimed particularly at the Negro market. This, it was argued, would sell not only records but, naturally enough, phonographs. One of these instruments could cost as little as ten dollars but, once bought, you needed constant supplies of needles, not to mention records. Buying the latest record became as much of a need then as it is now. This was good for record companies, but equally good for performers (exploitation apart), who found new audiences, especially in vaudeville, wanting to hear the real thing.

A Blues boom was born with the release of Mamie Smith's record *Crazy Blues* (1920) which sold over a million copies in its first six months and the amount of recorded Blues material from this decade is enormous. This is fortunate, for it allows us to hear not only the singers, but their accompanists, many of whom were as great, if not greater, in their own right.

The photographer photographed: Jimmy Rushing – Mr Five by Five – caught at London's Finsbury Park Astoria during a UK tour in the mid-1960s. Rushing was born in 1903 and is highly rated as a singer not only of the Urban Blues but also of a wide variety of other types of less specialized song. He first emerged with Walter Page's Blue Devils in 1927, sang with Bennie Moten 1929–35 and with Count Basie 1935–48. His empathy with the Basie band was such that he continued to work with them after he had taken off on his own. From the late 1950s, Rushing was associated with trumpeter Buck Clayton, after touring with his All Stars. He died of lukemia in 1972

MA RAINEY

The spiritual mother of female Blues singers was Gertrude 'Ma' Rainey, born in 1886. She first appeared in vaudeville in her native Columbus, Ohio, at the age of twelve; six years later she married William 'Pa' Rainey and the couple toured with the Rabbit Foot Minstrels. She first recorded in 1923 accompanied by Lovie Austin's Blues Serenaders, and went on to make a comparatively large number of records with many accompanists (including particularly Louis Armstrong, Coleman Hawkins, Tommy Ladnier and Joe Smith).

Ma Rainey's recording career ended in 1930; she toured until 1933 when her mother died and she retired to Rome (Ga). She died in 1939.

IDA COX

Continuing our parade in order of chronological seniority, we next encounter Ida Cox, born in Cedartown (Ga) in 1889. She ran away from home at the age of fourteen, also to join the Rabbit Foot Minstrels. Her career followed Ma Rainey's in the 1920s: she recorded first in 1923 (just before Ma), also with Lovie Austin, and continued a long recording career with a varied assortment of top musicians sympathetic to her style.

In 1927 she married the musician Jesse Crump, and went on tour with her own show. She continued to perform and record (in spite of a stroke in 1945) until the early 1960s; her health then deteriorated and she died in 1967.

BESSIE SMITH

Ma Rainey's chief protégée was undoubtedly Bessie Smith, born in Chattanooga (Tenn) in 1894; she was another Rabbit Foot Minstrel in her teens. She developed a majestic Vaudeville Blues style, but was virtually unknown until 1923 when the New Orleans pianist/composer Clarence Williams was sent to find her as the answer to the immensely popular Urban Blues singer Mamie Smith (no relation) whose 1920 recording of *Crazy Blues* had become a best seller.

Bessie's greatest years, when she became known as 'The Empress of the Blues', were that comparatively short period 1923–28 when she made a large number of recordings with a variety of accompanists, notably Louis Armstrong and James P. Johnson. After that, although she tried to adapt her

Ma Rainey – matriarch of Blues singers

style to public demand, she slipped from general favor, continuing a stormy and erratic career until she died in an automobile accident in 1937.

BERTHA CHIPPIE HILL

Another Ma Rainey protégée was Bertha 'Chippie' Hill, born in Charleston (SC) in about 1900. She sang with King Oliver in Chicago, and recorded with Louis Armstrong in the mid-1920s. She was more or less inactive between 1930 and 1946, but then was rediscovered and made further records and acclaimed appearances until her revitalized career was cut short by an automobile accident in 1950.

LIZZIE MILES

There are several other notable female singers, but most of them were not strictly Blues singers, and they appeared with larger bands (see Chapters 6 and 7). A prototype of such singers, who bridged the styles, so to speak, was Lizzie Miles, born in New Orleans in 1895. There she sang with early Jazz Bands; she toured the South, visited Europe, and performed and recorded with Jelly Roll Morton, King Oliver and Fats Waller in the 1920s and 1930s. She con-

The St. Louis Blues
(W. C. Handy)
BESSIE SMITH - Organ and
Cornet Accomp.
14064-D
(140241)
MADE AND PAT'D IN U.S.A. JAN. 21,'13 AND MAY 22,'23

Bessie Smith – the Empress of the Blues – stern and joyful

Blind Lemon Jefferson

tinued to be popular as an entertainer until her retirement in 1959; she died in 1963.

Almost all the male singers of the more Archaic Blues were also instrumentalists, as mentioned above. And the instrument is always one capable (in the right hands) of echoing and complementing the singer's voice – the guitar. (The harmonica is also capable of such impressions, but playing it precludes the performer's singing!) Possibly because they were able to provide their own accompaniments, male singers were freer of the influences which shifted the Archaic Blues from its roots. However, the more urbane the performers perforce became, the more their music was modified to the supposed needs of the public: it is a long way from Mahogany to Carnegie Hall.

BLIND LEMON JEFFERSON

Lemon Jefferson was born blind near Wortham (Texas) in the late 1870s. He early began singing and playing guitar and built up a rich repertoire of some of the most primitive Blues. In the mid-1910s he moved to Dallas, where he met and taught Leadbelly (see below); they played as a duo, Jefferson on Hawaiian guitar and Leadbelly on mandoline.

During the last five years of his chaotic life he recorded profusely, and it was after his last recording session, in the winter of 1930, that he became lost in a snowstorm; the next day, he was found frozen to death.

LEADBELLY

Leadbelly (*né* Huddie Ledbetter) was born in Mooringsport (La) in 1885, and brought up in Texas. He was a rough and violent man, and served three prison sentences: for murder, attempted murder, and assault. Not surprisingly, this roughness came through in his singing, especially in his recreation of prison Work Songs.

We have already mentioned his association with Blind Lemon Jefferson, much of whose work was as rough as his. Leadbelly played a 12-string guitar: his repertoire ranging from the authentically Negro to the worst pop ballads. He was one of the folk singers encouraged to perform and record by John and Alan Lomax, indefatigable collectors, for whom he was chauffeur for a time.

In the 1940s he played in clubs and toured, but was held in higher esteem by his audiences than by his fellow musicians. He died in 1949.

LONNIE JOHNSON

Lonnie Johnson, born in New Orleans (La) in about 1889, was as much a Jazz musician as a folk guitarist, but he did play and sing some very fine Blues. He studied the violin and played the piano as well as the guitar. After an early visit to London he worked on the riverboats until the mid-1920s, when he started recording as the result of his winning first prize in a Blues contest in St Louis. From the early 1930s until his death in 1970 his career moved in and out of music. Some of his best work is to be heard with Armstrong, Ellington, the guitarist Eddie Lang, and as an accompanist to Blues singers, including himself.

Leadbelly and 12-string guitar

Lonnie Johnson

Big Bill Broonzy

BIG BILL BROONZY

One of the most prolific and authentic (subject to the usual provisos) Blues singers and guitarists was Big Bill Broonzy, born in Scott (Miss) in 1893. His musical career started on a home-made violin; it was not until the early 1920s, when he moved to Chicago, that he learned to play the guitar under the tutelage of Papa Charlie Jackson.

By the mid-1920s he was making records, and his powerful authenticity raised him to the ranks of the best sellers, and by the early 1940s he was one of the lucky musicians able to make a living by his art alone. In the early 1950s he toured Europe, received as a legendary folk hero, but the end of the decade saw his health declining and he died of cancer in 1958.

JOSH WHITE

Even non-purists would recognize that much of Josh White's work is a long way from the roots of Blues, but at the same time there is enough to ensure his inclusion here. White was born in Greenville (sc) in 1908; his father was a preacher and his musical career began in the music of the church. Later, he acted as guide to Blind Lemon Jefferson, who greatly influenced his music. He moved to New York, where he first recorded in the early 1930s; toward the end of the decade he became a night-club performer of increasing popularity. This had its effect on his repertoire, for he used his art to comment on

Josh White

racial matters. In the 1950s he toured Europe, where he was as popular as Broonzy, to whom he formed an interesting contrast. In 1966 he retired from music after a car accident; he died three years later.

SONNY TERRY AND BROWNIE McGHEE

These two artists have to be mentioned in the same breath, as they have been associated as a duo since 1939. Terry was born in Durham (NC) in 1911 and became blind in his teens; it was in hospital at this time that he learned to play the harmonica. This he plays in a unique imitation of the human voice, interspersed with equally individual vocal effects.

McGhee was born in Knoxville (Tenn) in 1915, and was taught to play guitar by his father. Since joining forces with Sonny Terry in 1939 the two have toured the world and appeared in numerous films and shows. It says much for their artistic integrity that their performance has remained peculiarly rural in spite of commercial pressures.

MUDDY WATERS

The guitarist/singer Muddy Waters was born in Rolling Fork (Miss) in 1915. He was discovered by collector Alan Lomax and made some Library of Congress recordings in the early 1940s; shortly after this he worked as a night-club artist in Chicago, and started to make commercial recordings toward the end of that decade.

He has toured highly successfully from the late 1950s, and has also led bands which produce tremendously exciting Blues. Not the least of his achievements has been his influence on the course of Pop music, via the late Jimi Hendrix and the Rolling Stones – to whom he indirectly gave their name. Although Muddy Waters uses an amplified guitar, and the 'bottle-neck' style of playing to which we referred earlier, he has resisted the debasement of his work by commercial pressures, while remaining highly successful.

It is clear that there are several strands of Blues co-existing, and fortunately we have an uninterrupted stream of recordings reaching back over 60 years from which to make comparisons. The Rural Blues are to be heard from such past performers as Leadbelly, Broonzy, and from such present-day exponents as Sonny Terry and Brownie McGhee. Urban or Vaudeville Blues may be heard from the ladies of the Rabbit Foot

Sonny Terry and Brownie McGhee – inseparable Blues Duo

Muddy Waters – concentration and enthusiasm

Minstrels and others. A few well-known examples from Bessie Smith are *Sam Jones Blues*, *Kitchen Man*, *Nobody Knows You When You're Down and Out* and *Need a Little Sugar in My Bowl*. Jazz Blues covers a whole range of work from (for example) Jelly Roll Morton's *Buddy Bolden's Blues* to *Royal Garden Blues* by Clarence and Spencer Williams.

No chapter on the Blues would be complete without a reference to the much-maligned W. C. Handy. Handy was born in Florence (Ala) in 1873, had a musical training, and started to tour with a minstrel band at the turn of the century. He was one of the first trained musicians to 'discover' the Blues form and to write down examples, and to the performers this was his crime – he was stealing their music. Handy did for the Blues what Cecil Sharp did for English folk song – with, one must admit, as much lack of sympathy and understanding on occasion. Among the many Blues which he wrote down, composed, arranged, or published, the best known are *Careless (Loveless) Love* and *St Louis Blues*. Handy turned to music publishing in New York in the early 1920s, and continued to work, though blind for about the last twenty years of his life, until his death in 1957.

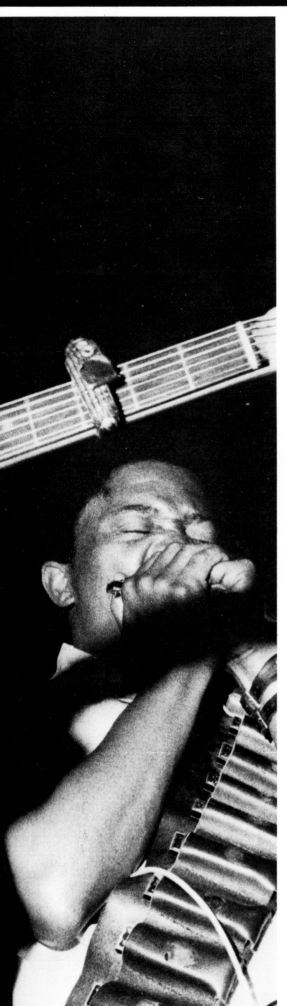

William Henry Joseph Bonaparte Bertholoff (1897–1973), known as Willie 'The Lion' (from his bravery in the First World War) Smith (the name of his stepfather). The Lion was one of the pioneers of the Harlem Stride piano style, with a personality and 'props' (bowler and cigar) comparable with those of the equally great but considerably less durable Fats Waller

4/PIANO JAZZ

Although our discussion of musicians and their music so far has in some cases taken us up almost to the present day, we must not lose sight of the fact that our starting points were two distinct types of music which existed in America at the turn of the century. On the one hand, we had what we chose to call New Orleans Jazz, a synthesis of the brass band and Ragtime styles. On the other, we had the Blues, which owed little to anything except its African roots, via the work songs.

But that was at the turn of the century. If one stream of the Blues managed to remain free from the influence of New Orleans Jazz, it was less easy for Jazz to avoid absorbing the Blues into its development. One reason for this was that there is nothing to stop a Jazz band playing around the (12-bar) Blues sequence. Another reason was that when musicians accompanied Blues singers they were forced to adopt an appropriate style – often part of their musical heritage anyway – which they then carried back to their Jazz playing. However, one influence on New Orleans Jazz which we have often mentioned but not yet described remained undisturbed – Ragtime.

Ragtime is another word with various meanings. Referring to a minstrel music which focussed itself on the piano in the 1890s, it has taken on a particular meaning which distinguishes that music from the Jazz of the musicians

Mary Lou Williams, pictured here in prewar days, is doubtless the most important and certainly the most active Jazzwoman. Born in 1910, she still plays all styles of Jazz piano with remarkable energy, and has half a century of recordings to her credit, not to mention a formidable array of compositions and arrangements for many leading bands, including Armstrong, Ellington and Goodman

described above. In fact the word Ragtime was probably a general term for Jazz before the latter was coined, but here we are talking about the piano style which has recently enjoyed a popular revival, particularly under the precise and magical fingers of Joshua Rifkin, following the use of Scott Joplin's *The Entertainer* (1902) as theme music for the film *The Sting* (1973).

Since, unlike most emerging music of the period, much Ragtime was committed to paper, and also to piano-rolls, we have here a unique opportunity to examine an area of musical development at first hand.

Ragtime contains elements both of the march and of European music, developed via the 'Coon Songs' of the minstrel schools and that popular dance, the Cakewalk. Early Jazz bands played Ragtime but it became particularly identified with the piano and developed separately on that instrument for obvious practical reasons – whoever heard of a piano in a marching band?

The piano has always been a popular instrument in the home, not least because of its ability to make music at the hands of one performer. The piano was – and is – an instrument widely taught and learnt, with an enormous repertoire of written music of all sorts. It is no accident that many of the composers, arrangers and bandleaders we shall later meet were pianists.

Nat King Cole (1917–65) was a Hines-influenced pianist whose importance in that role was overshadowed by his success as a singer. His trio – with Oscar Moore (gtr) and Wesley Prince (bass) – was widely known in the early 1940s, but by the end of that decade he was to be found singing romantic ballads with big bands; a long way from Jazz. He also acted and performed in several movies, notably as W C Handy in the biographical *St Louis Blues*

SCOTT JOPLIN

The name of Scott Joplin, for reasons mentioned above, is nowadays popularly synonymous with Ragtime, but there were many pioneers before him to lay the foundation of his success, and many other composers and performers. Louis Chauvin (1880–1908), for example, although little is left from his short life other than the memories of those who heard him, must be reckoned with as a performer to whom Joplin owes a debt. Tom Turpin (1873–1922) too, who owned the Rosebud Saloon in St Louis, and there provided some focus for the development of a St Louis Ragtime school, was in the top rank of composers and performers, and is credited with one of the first published Rags: *Harlem Rag* (1897).

Joplin was born into a musical family in Texarkana (Texas) in 1868; he started to teach himself piano at an early age and his achievements so impressed a local music teacher that he is said to have given the young musician free lessons. Joplin clearly had some idea of where he was going, as he left home at the age of fourteen to become a performer of the music which was beginning to shape itself into what would later be called 'Ragtime' – performing with his own group at the Chicago World Fair in 1893.

He then moved to Sedalia (Mo), where he met the entrepreneur John Stark, who became his music publisher, and to whom he owed much of his success. In 1898, Stark published Joplin's *Original Rags* and *Maple Leaf Rag*; the latter became an instant success. These were followed by dozens of others, but Joplin's aspirations for 'his' music were more advanced. He went on to compose full-scale works such as the Ragtime opera *A Guest of Honor* (performed in 1903, but never published) and *Treemonisha* (1911). Both were failures, and the complete lack of recognition which the latter received did nothing to encourage the unhappy Joplin; his health took a turn for the worse, and he did little more before dying in 1917, at about the end of the Ragtime craze.

Thomas 'Fats' Waller

The development of Ragtime in its 'classical' form was left to a few masters. Its contribution to the development of Jazz was the inspiration it gave to many other pianists to adapt it so that the piano could enter the Jazz bands which had hitherto managed without that instrument. We have already seen how Jelly Roll Morton made his contribution to Jazz by the extension and adaptation of his Ragtime beginnings, and there were many others who developed the style in their own way.

Before we look at some of them, however, we should say a few words about the name itself – Piano Jazz – and dispel the idea which somewhere gained currency that it is impossible to play Jazz on the piano. Certainly if you define Jazz in a particularly narrow way, so as to exclude the piano, the contention must be true, but no one would surely accept such a definition. Another factor sometimes held to exclude the piano is that it arrived in the Jazz band so late. Perhaps it is forgotten that it did arrive before the saxophone. . . .

Scott Joplin about 1911

JAMES P JOHNSON

James P. Johnson was born in New Brunswick (NJ) in 1891 and studied piano from an early age. The family moved to New York where he met Luckey Roberts, a Ragtime pianist who owned a bar in Harlem. It was here that Johnson was inspired to develop Ragtime into a style which became known as (Harlem) stride, in which the striding is performed by the left hand, turning the

James P. Johnson

regularity of Ragtime into something much more free.

Johnson toured the US in vaudeville, and visited Europe as the musical director of a roadshow in the 1920s. At that time, his excellence as a pianist was often overlooked since he devoted much of his energy to musical composition and direction. However, his recordings, notably those with Bessie Smith, show his great capability and sympathy as soloist and accompanist. He continued to compose and play until 1940, when he had a stroke. This limited his ability to work, but he continued until a paralyzing stroke in 1951 left him immobile and unable to speak; he died in 1955.

He was the inspiration for many other pianists: those who took the stride piano and developed it in their own ways – Duke Ellington, for example – and one in particular who became as much a symbol of ebullient musicianship as of Jazz, Fats Waller.

FATS WALLER

Waller was born in New York in 1904. His father, a church minister, hoped that his son would follow in his footsteps; his mother played the piano and organ, which her son studied. By the age of fifteen, Waller had become a professional pianist in cabarets and theaters and started to record in the 1920s, not only on the piano but also the organ – one of the few and certainly the first to make the latter an instrument of Jazz.

The development of Waller's style from that of James P. Johnson (who taught him informally) can be clearly heard: Waller's left hand was so powerful that he needed no rhythm section.

Waller was able to hold his own as a popular entertainer without debasing the Jazz he played – no mean feat considering that much of his best-known work is a conscious parody and self-parody of Tin Pan Alley songs. And although he was not a singer, he turned that very deficiency to good use in his guying entertainment.

He toured the US and visited England in 1938, where he made a great impact on music-hall audiences. But he lived hard, and drank hard, and was found dead in a railway sleeping car at Kansas City while travelling to New York City from Los Angeles in 1943.

EARL HINES

Earl Hines was born in Duquesne (Pa) in 1905, of a musical family; his mother, like Fats Waller's, was an organist. He studied the piano in the hope of becoming a concert

Earl 'Fatha' Hines

pianist, but turned toward Jazz and moved to Chicago where he met Louis Armstrong. Hines developed a unique style, inspired by Armstrong and known as the 'trumpet style': his right hand playing runs and tremolos in a way which was quite unlike anything which had ever been heard before. Not surprisingly, Hines was the spiritual father of many other Jazz pianists, but his innovation was so advanced for its time that although it hardly changed through several decades it remained fresh and never seemed outdated.

In the 1930s, he led big bands and, looking back, must find satisfaction in having nurtured many outstanding musicians, including Dizzy Gillespie and Charlie Parker. Apart from a spell on tour with Louis Armstrong's All Stars, Hines has continued to play both solo and as a leader with an undiminished vigor which has led some to claim him the greatest Jazz pianist ever.

BOOGIE WOOGIE

The styles of the Jazz pianists we have met so far – and of those yet to come – are derived from Ragtime. Boogie was derived from a different source – the Blues guitarists. It follows the 12-bar Blues sequence (see Appendix 1) and its characteristic is a driving, repetitive, 8-to-the-bar bass figure. Above this figure, the right hand plays riffs, developed chorus by chorus.

Where the name Boogie came from is uncertain, but there is little doubt that it first became known through Clarence 'Pinetop' Smith's recording *Pinetop's Boogie Woogie* (Chicago, 1928). The style, however, is much older than this first recording of it; some attribute it to Cow Cow Davenport.

Pinetop Smith was accidentally shot in a nightclub altercation, in which he had no part, in 1929. To what heights he might have risen had he lived is a matter for speculation; one suspects that he might have said it all in his few recordings. There were, however, many other practitioners of the art of Boogie who were either natives of, or had gravitated toward, the Chicago of the 1920s, but at that time they were poor and unknown.

In the hands of masters, Boogie can be tremendously exciting, but its simplicity is deceptive. Its basic monotony means that only the best players can hold our interest, and it may be no coincidence that Boogie and Swing (see Chapter 7) rose together, the latter helping to deflower the former.

Boogie remains captured in its proper – though often earthy – innocence by a few performers who were able to play it without debasing it.

Jimmy Yancey

JIMMY YANCEY

For delicate Boogie, rich in its Blues influence, turn to Jimmy Yancey, born in Chicago (Ill) in 1894, son of a vaudeville guitarist and singer. Yancey was a child prodigy, a tap-dancer who, by the age of ten, had toured the US from coast to coast and by twenty had completed a two-year tour of Europe and retired from the stage.

He started to teach himself to play the piano at the age of fifteen and entertained regularly until, seeking greater security than the musical life offered, he retired to become a groundsman at Comiskey Park, home of

Meade 'Lux' Lewis

the Chicago White Sox. He was held in high esteem by his fellow pianists, and was persuaded from his musical retirement to take part in the Boogie boom in the late 1930s, making several records of rare delicacy and appearing at a Carnegie Hall concert in 1948. He died in 1951.

Yancey made many memorable and moving recordings with his wife, singer Estella 'Mama' Yancey, though in some his accompaniment is more competitive than complementary. Some have called Jimmy Yancey 'the Father of Boogie Woogie' and though this is not really a valid title, he had not a little influence on the Chicago Boogie pianists, and has a secure place in the development of the style.

MEADE LUX LEWIS

Meade Lux Lewis was born in Chicago (Ill) in 1905, but spent his childhood in Louisville (Ky), where he learnt the violin. Returning to Chicago, he met Jimmy Yancey and was inspired to play the piano, subsequently becoming a night-club pianist. In 1929 he made a record of his *Honky Tonk Train Blues*, but the Depression forced him into the obscurity of a succession of laboring jobs. However, when the Jazz critic and entrepreneur John Hammond heard that record in 1935, he set out to find Lewis, thus laying the foundations of the unexpected Boogie boom and the Carnegie Hall concerts.

Lewis is chiefly remembered through records of his various Boogie solos, particularly the developing *Honky Tonk Train Blues*, and for his three-piano work with Albert Ammons and Pete Johnson. He left their company in the early 1940s and settled in Los Angeles, but continued to tour and to record until his untimely death in a car crash in 1964.

PETE JOHNSON

Pete Johnson was born in Kansas City (Mo) in 1904, started his musical career as a drummer, and turned to the piano in his late teens. In the 1920s he met bartender 'Big Joe' Turner who, starting his singing career with Johnson, went on to fame as a Blues shouter in his own right, though he continued to appear with Johnson for many years. The two stayed in Kansas City until 1938, when they appeared with Benny Goodman on a New York radio show, and were taken up by John Hammond for the Boogie boom.

Johnson worked on and off to the end of

Pete Johnson

the 1940s, particularly with Albert Ammons; toured until 1953 and then retired to Buffalo (NY). He still made occasional appearances and recordings and toured Europe in 1958, but he had a heart attack at the end of that year and never recovered his health; he died in 1967.

Although he was known as one of the foremost Boogie pianists, Johnson had a much wider range of styles than his colleagues.

ALBERT AMMONS

Ammons was born in Chicago (Ill) in 1907, and associated early with Meade Lux Lewis, Pinetop Smith and Jimmy Yancey, developing one of the most powerful Boogie styles of them all.

He formed his own band in the early 1930s, based in Chicago until his John Hammond-inspired move to New York in 1938 with the Boogie boom. Many of his

performances during this New York period were duets with Pete Johnson, but he also appeared and recorded with many other artists, adapting the Boogie style to other music, not always with happy results. After his New York sojourn he returned to Chicago, but although he continued his musical career it was interrupted by ill health and he died in 1949.

5/WHITE JAZZ

The veteran Papa Laine's Children at a recording session in New Orleans in 1951 – Dr Ed Souchon (gtr), Baduc (dms), Johnny Wiggs (tpt), Mendelson (pno), Harry Shields (clt), Tom Brown (tmb), Mangiapane (bass)

t is a sore point for many purists that the first band to make a record of Jazz was made up of White musicians: the Original Dixieland Jazz Band (ODJB). The truth is that there were White musicians in New Orleans as everywhere else, that they had their own marching bands, and that they played Jazz.

The general term Dixie dates at least from the mid-nineteenth century, and applied to the southern states of the US; it derived possibly from the word Dix which appeared on the ten-dollar bills issued by a Francophile bank in New Orleans. The name Dixie Music was applied at the turn of the century to what we would now call New Orleans Jazz. The change in name from Dixie to Jazz must have occurred in the years 1910–15, when the ODJB appeared. Because the word Dixieland became particularly attached to that band, which happened to be White, its more general meaning was largely forgotten and it came to be applied, sometimes in a derogatory and dismissive way, to White Jazz.

Anyone who does use the term Dixieland for White Jazz should pause to wonder why King Oliver named his 1925 band the Dixie Syncopators, why Coleman Hawkins described Jelly Roll Morton's music as 'Dixieland,' and why Jay Jay Johnson applied the same description to Kid Ory's. Even if we allow a certain contorted logic to assert that both Hawkins and Johnson were (independently) being as rude as possible to Morton and Ory, it would hardly explain Oliver's deliberate use of the word to describe his own band.

Right: The British trumpeter Pat Halcox with tenorman Bud Freeman at the Manchester Jazz Festival, 1962

Tony Spargo (*né* Sbarbaro, 1897–1969) – longest surviving member of the ODJB

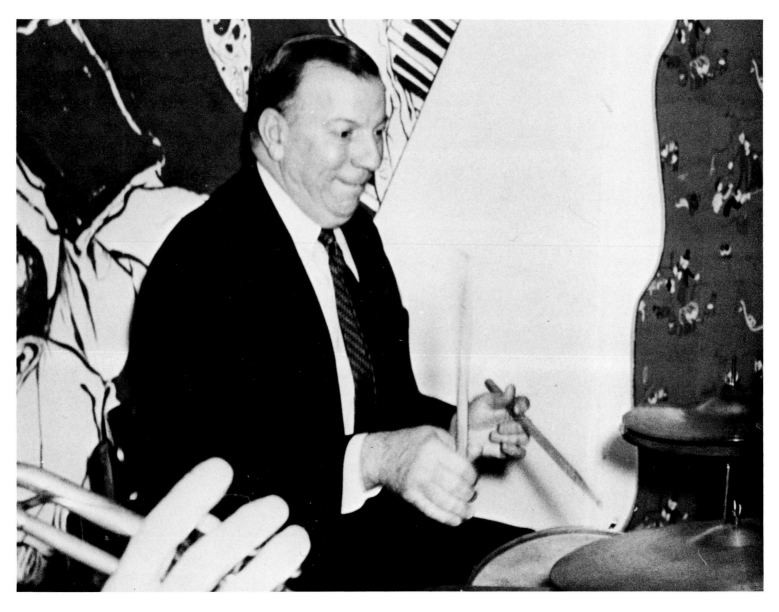

ODJB

Papa Jack Laine was born in New Orleans (La) in 1873. He formed his first band at the age of fifteen, playing marches and the emerging Ragtime music. He continued to lead and organize bands, notably the Reliance Brass Band in the 1900s whose cornettist, Nick La Rocca, became the cornerstone of the ODJB.

Bands have always thrived on interchanging personnel: the arrival of new musicians with new ideas helps to keep the music fresh. This ever-changing scene, while it makes the life of the historian more difficult, underlines the fact that the individual musician in Jazz has far more importance, generally, than his counterpart in other fields of musical expression.

The ODJB was formed in 1916 after a disagreement amongst the members of Stein's Dixie Jass Band; the new leader was cornettist Nick La Rocca, with Larry Shields (clarinet), Eddie Edwards (trombone), Henry Ragas (piano) and Tony Spargo (drums). The following year, this was the band which made the first recordings of Jazz.

The photograph here shows the ODJB which visited London in 1919. Emil Christian had replaced Eddie Edwards on trombone, and Russell Robinson had replaced Henry Ragas on piano. The tour was not without difficulty: the band was booked to appear in the musical revue *Joy Bells* but lasted for one performance only as the star, George Robey, was upstaged (he thought) and got rid of them. The ODJB soon recovered from this setback and continued the tour, predictably giving rise to wildly mixed reactions from the critics. However, they played a Command

The ODJB in London, 1919 – Russell Robinson (pno), Larry Shields (clt), Nick La Rocca (tpt), Emil Christian (tmb), Tony Spargo (dms)

Performance before King George V, and appeared at the 1919 Victory Ball, before returning to the USA the following year, leaving a legacy of the first Jazz recordings to be made in Britain, and an inspired younger generation with a widened gap between it and its parents.

NORK

The other acronymic pioneering White band was the New Orleans Rhythm Kings (or Friars' Society Orchestra as it was first called) which first appeared at the Friars' Inn, Chicago, in 1921, and disbanded in 1924.

The leader was trumpeter Paul Mares, born in New Orleans in 1900, who moved to Chicago via the riverboats. After his period with NORK he virtually retired from music, became a Chicago restauranteur, and died in 1949.

The outstanding members of NORK were the clarinettist and trombonist, Leon Roppolo and George Brunis. Brunis was born in New Orleans in 1900, played with Papa Laine, and moved to Chicago in 1919. After his sojourn with NORK, he recorded sympathetically with Bix Beiderbecke; then (by way of a contrast) toured for over ten years with Ted Lewis. He spent the rest of his life leading, or making an essential contribution to, Dixieland groups until his death in 1974. Apart from being the first White tailgate trombonist, and a stage clown who could operate the trombone slide with his foot, he also advanced the art of sympathetic Jazz trombone playing.

Leon Roppolo (or Rappolo) was born into a musical family in Lutheran (La) in 1902. He was a highly gifted, self-taught

NORK in 1923, including Paul Mares (tpt), Leon Roppolo (clt), George Brunis (tmb), Steve Brown (bass) and Ben Pollack (dms)

clarinet player, and ran away from home in his early teens to tour in vaudeville. The high spot of his career was his period with NORK; shortly afterwards, his mind failed and he spent most of the rest of his life – he died in 1943 – in a mental hospital.

NORK's drummer was Ben Pollack, born in Chicago in 1903. After NORK, he formed his own band which acted as a nursery for many of the leaders of the next decade, including Bud Freeman, Benny Goodman, Harry James, Glenn Miller, Muggsy Spanier and Jack Teagarden. From the 1940s, Pollack became more of an entrepreneur than a performer, finally leaving music altogether to become, like Mares, a restauranteur. He committed suicide in 1971.

Right: Ben Pollack (seated) and his Orchestra

Below right: The Austin High School Gang about 1926 – Frankie Trumbauer (alt), Jim Lanigan (bass), Bud Freeman (ten), Jimmy McPartland (tpt), Dave Tough (dms), Floyd O'Brien (tmb), Dave North (pno), Dick McPartland (bjo)

Below: George Brunis

THE AUSTIN HIGH SCHOOL GANG

From time to time a group of musicians comes together which contains a variety of emerging talent – which is not the same thing as a group of established, talented musicians deciding to join forces. Such was the Austin High School Gang, formed in the early 1920s in Chicago, with such luminaries as Bud Freeman, Dick and Jimmy McPartland, Frank Teschemacher and Dave Tough.

Born in Chicago in 1903, Freeman was the first and certainly one of the finest tenor sax players of Dixieland, often compared and contrasted with Coleman Hawkins and Lester Young. During a long and distin-guished career he has played and recorded with many of the other undisputed greats of Jazz.

The McPartland brothers' father was a Chicago music teacher who taught not only Bud Freeman, but also his own sons Dick and Jimmy. Dick was born in 1905, studied violin and later banjo and guitar, the latter with such effect that he was able to take over from Eddie Lang in the Mound City Blue Blowers. He was forced to retire from music because of ill health and died in 1957. Jimmy, born in 1907, also learned violin and later cornet; a disciple of Bix Beiderbecke he took over from him in the Wolverines. He has continued to play, teach and tour extensively.

Frank Teschemacher was born in Kansas

Bud Freeman

City (Mo) in 1906 but moved to Chicago, where his clarinet playing was inspired by Johnny Dodds and Jimmie Noone. He was acknowledged as one of the greatest musicians of his school, but his career was cut short by an automobile accident in which he met his death in 1932.

Dave Tough was born in Oak Park (Ill) in 1908. He was a drummer of the first rank, inspired by Baby Dodds. His career was continually interrupted by illness; his greatest periods were with the Chicago musicians

Jimmy McPartland

Dave Tough

Bix & Tram

Frankie Trumbauer

Bix Beiderbecke

Red Nichols

at the end of the 1920s and during the Swing Era with Tommy Dorsey, Benny Goodman, and Jack Teagarden. He died after a fall in 1948.

BIX BEIDERBECKE

Bix Beiderbecke was born in Davenport (Ia) in 1903; he started to learn the piano at the age of three and the cornet at fourteen. His introduction to Jazz came from the riverboats which steamed as far as Davenport, and was influenced by the riverboat trumpeter Emmett Hardy. At the age of twenty he joined the Wolverines and played in New York, then Chicago, where he absorbed all he could from Armstrong and Oliver. In 1926 he met Frankie Trumbauer, the C-melody saxophonist, who worked with him in St Louis. He then worked with Jean Goldkette and Paul Whiteman. Trumbauer stayed with Whiteman until the mid-1930s, but Bix became more and more unreliable through alcoholism, and left Whiteman in 1930. He died the following year.

Bix is probably one of the most discussed Jazz musicians of his time; certainly he is held in a very high regard in which legend and performance are intertwined. There is no doubt that he made a significant contribution to Jazz, and that his inspiration lived on in Jimmy McPartland, Red Nichols, Bobby Hackett and Rex Stewart. It is also interesting to listen to his piano composition *In a Mist*, and to reflect that it was recorded in the same year as the first Hot 5 sessions.

Birthday celebration of the Duke Ellington
Orchestra; seated next to Duke is singer Ivie Anderson

6/BIG BANDS

When is a band big? How long is a piece of string? When a band is small, and all its musicians know the tunes – Jazz standards – there is little difficulty in co-ordination. Its musicians work to the chord sequences (see Appendix 1) and develop, by experience, a musical rapport which enables them to improvise upon these sequences. Many of the early musicians were unable to read music, and even today some amateurs are musically illiterate – often making a virtue of it. But the idea of improvisation as something sacred or magical in itself is misleading, for the players are constrained by the tune, or its chord sequence, and there are few who do not play the same 'improvised' solo time after time for any given tune.

We have already met Jelly Roll Morton as the first great Jazz composer/arranger, and it is to composition and arrangement we must look for our next development. Composition is not merely writing the melodic line of a tune; it is also necessary to indicate how it is to be harmonized. Although this is part of the act of composition, it must be done with some line-up of instru-

Bill Coleman and Ben Webster

Duke Ellington urges trumpeter Cat Anderson to hit one of his famed high notes during a UK concert in the mid-1960s

ments in mind, in other words, arranged for a particular combination of sounds. But arrangement is not just that: as well as being a part of composition it may be a separate act in that the arranger takes an existing piece and adapts it for another combination of instruments.

The emergence of the composer/arranger – for the two arts are closely bound – had two effects. The first was that musicians who could read music became the rule rather than the exception. The second was that bands increased in size: once the full possibilities of arrangement had struck home, arrangers needed a larger canvas on which to paint – and thus the Big Band was born. Instead of one trumpet, one trombone, and so on, *sections* of two or three of each instrument were introduced. Within a section there might be a *featured soloist* – an outstanding musician for whose improvisational talent the arranger could allow. Otherwise, the ordinary *sideman* would be a good reader who could interpret the intentions of the arranger to give the band its individual sound. Some musicians would *double* on other instruments, giving the whole an even greater flexibility.

Inevitably, some saw such developments as the death of Jazz, and if Jazz is collective improvisation that must be true. On the other hand, the Big Band was a natural development, and provided an extended and more varied repertoire: a wider-than-ever base for improvisation. It has also been suggested that the advent of 'written Jazz' was an imposition of Western culture, or orthodoxy, on an art form which had sprung from a different stock. But the technique of written music was freely chosen by many Jazz composers and arrangers, and their satisfaction with the resulting performances (which they often directed as leaders of the bands) suggests that the development was welcomed rather than resented as a restriction of creative freedom. Certainly, few would deny Fletcher Henderson, Duke Ellington, and many others who worked in this way their contributions to the world of Jazz.

Whatever the arguments, there is no denying that the 1920s saw the advent of the composer/arranger – often a multi-instrumentalist, often a pianist – and that a new era, a new sound in Jazz, was born: that of the Big Band. This development could and did lead to some fusion, and confusion, between Jazz and dance bands. To be respectable, a Jazz band might call itself a dance band – or orchestra, an even more acceptable word. To be daring, a dance orchestra might pretend to play Jazz. It may have been such activities which provided first-class whetstones for the axes of the purists. If there are any purists of this type still about, let them remember Jazz pioneer Jelly Roll Morton's words:

You'd please me if you'd just play those little black dots – just those little black dots that I put down there. If you play them, you'll please me. You don't have to make a lot of noise and ad-lib. All I want you to play is what's written. That's all I ask.

It usually comes as a shock to the novice to find that the first of the great composer/arrangers for Jazz was Jelly Roll Morton, and that the Red Hot Peppers were not a splendidly free, improvising group but a tightly-controlled, well-rehearsed band playing just what their leader demanded. But perhaps the fact that such a free-sounding result is obtainable in such strict circumstances should give us heart.

The 1920s, then, saw the birth of the Big Band, with sections of players rather than individuals, but players who were often known to be jazzmen – Bix Beiderbecke in The Paul Whiteman Orchestra, for example – rather than ordinary musicians.

PAUL WHITEMAN

Whiteman was born in Denver (Colo) in 1890, and during the 1920s rose to fame by his purveying of Symphonic Jazz – which included commissioning and performing George Gershwin's *Rhapsody in Blue*. As if this were not enough for those who insist that Gershwin's piece has nothing to do with the Blues, Whiteman and his Orchestra went on to make a film, *King of Jazz* (1930), following which the royal title adhered to Whiteman, infuriating those who insist that he also had nothing to do with Jazz. It is true that the Orchestra may have compared ill with its contemporaries, but it nurtured such jazzmen as Bix Beiderbecke and Frankie Trumbauer; the Dorseys; Eddie Lang and Joe Venuti; and Red Norvo. Whiteman continued as a musical entrepreneur until the 1950s, and died in 1967.

Whatever may be said about Whiteman (and a great deal is), he introduced a wide public to what they thought was Jazz, and, even if it was not, it must have made that public more receptive to the real thing.

MILDRED BAILEY

One of the features of any Big Band was its singer, and Mildred Bailey was one of the first girl singers; she was with Paul Whiteman from 1929–36. Mildred was born in Tekoa (Wash) in 1907, and was introduced to the Whiteman Orchestra by her brother Al who, with Harry Barris and Bing Crosby, had sung with Whiteman as the Rhythm Boys. Inspired by Bessie Smith, Mildred Bailey was the first white Jazz singer to gain acceptance; she in her turn influenced other singers such as Ella Fitzgerald and Peggy Lee. Mildred Bailey married Whiteman's xylophonist, Red Norvo, in 1933; they left Whiteman and worked together for some

Mildred Bailey

years, parting in 1945. She sang as a solo artiste with many other bands, but towards the end of the 1940s her health deteriorated and she died in 1951.

FLETCHER HENDERSON

Henderson was a pianist and bandleader, already mentioned as an employer of talented jazzmen. In fact he was the first to demonstrate the role of the leader, first as a talent-spotter, then as one who could make use of that talent by producing arrangements suited to it. This quality must be borne in mind when we consider what makes a great leader, and it applies to all those we encounter in our journey through the world of Jazz.

Henderson was born in Cuthbert (Ga) in 1898, graduated in chemistry and mathematics, and moved to New York in 1920 to pursue postgraduate studies. However, like many scientists, he was musically inclined, and instead of pursuing his studies, he started work as a song demonstrator; he then formed a band to accompany Ethel Waters on tour. By the mid-1920s, Henderson had the first Big Band to make a name in Jazz, which he led for a decade. A continual stream of luminaries passed through it, the most famous of whom was Louis Armstrong in 1924–25. During this time he also made countless records as accompanist to Blues singers, including notably Ma Rainey, and the non-related Bessie, Mamie and Trixie

Jack Teagarden

Smith. By the mid-1930s, Henderson's orchestra had fallen from favor, overtaken by those to whom he had shown the way. He joined Benny Goodman, for whom he had written arrangements, as pianist in 1939, but this was not where his talent lay and he left to form his own band again – though this venture was not very successful. The 1940s saw him dividing his time between band leading, arranging and accompanying; in 1948–49 he toured with Ethel Waters – his career had come full circle. The following year he had a stroke, and spent the last two years of his life inactive, dying as 1952 drew to a close.

DON REDMAN

Henderson came to arranging in the mid-1930s, some time after his musical career had begun. His early arrangements for the Big Band had been made by reedsman Don Redman, born in Piedmont (WVa) in 1900. Redman was a multi-instrumentalist, a child prodigy, who joined Henderson in 1924 and became the first notable Big Band arranger. It was he who introduced the Big Band 'sounds' which we now take for granted – such as sustained saxophone harmonies – and who combined lines written for particular musicians with the opportunity for improvisation. Redman left Henderson for McKinney's Cotton Pickers in 1927; in 1931 he took over the band of Horace Henderson (Fletcher's brother) and ran it until 1940. After that he spent most of his time arranging and directing until his death in 1964.

Fletcher Henderson

Ethel Waters

Don Redman

Paul Whiteman (ninth from left) and his 25-piece Orchestra

The Duke Ellington Orchestra

DUKE ELLINGTON

The most illustrious and indefatigable contributor to the world of Jazz, Duke Ellington, was born in Washington (DC) in 1899. Although he learned the piano from the age of seven, he does not seem to have shown any early signs of his outstanding musical ability, and was set on a career in sign-writing until his late teens. However, he did organize bands as a spare-time activity, and moved to New York in the early 1920s where he was inspired by the Harlem pianists James P. Johnson, Willie 'the Lion' Smith, and Fats Waller. It was Waller who persuaded Ellington back to New York (after his return to Washington) where, after various vicissitudes, he opened at the Kentucky Club and then moved to the Cotton Club in 1927, the start of his real fame.

By this time, he had such excellent sidemen as trumpeter Bubber Miley, trombonist Tricky Sam Nanton and baritone saxophonist Harry Carney. The band started to record and broadcast, and become nationally known. Miley, master of the mutes, was with Ellington from 1925–29. Nanton and Carney, however, who both joined in 1926, stayed until their deaths, Nanton in 1948 and Carney, who outlived Ellington and remained in the orchestra led by his son Mercer Ellington, in 1974 – a record. Many other musicians stayed with Ellington for long periods, for example, Barney Bigard, clarinettist from 1928–42; Johnny Hodges, alto player 1928–51 and 1955 until his death in 1970; Cootie Williams, trumpeter, who succeeded Miley, 1929–40 and 1962–75, into the Mercer Era. Notable also was singer Ivie Anderson, who sang with Ellington from 1931 to 1942, when she was forced to retire by ill health.

All this shows the tremendous rapport between Ellington and his musicians; if there is such a thing as job satisfaction in the Jazz

Johnny Hodges

world, it must have been here. From 1930, the Ellington Orchestra began to enjoy an ever-widening popularity, with success after success flowing from the prolific pen of its leader. In 1939 Ellington was joined by the pianist, composer and arranger Billy Stray-horn, with whom he thenceforward worked so intimately and with such rapport that their styles became indistinguishable. While other leaders' popularity and output varied over the years, Ellington's never diminished: he wrote innumerable scores of the highest quality, toured the world and had scores of honors heaped upon him; he was truly the giant of Jazz. He continued to work until, interrupted by ill health in his last few months, he died in 1974. The orchestra continued under his son, Mercer Ellington.

Duke Ellington

Barney Bigard

Harry Carney

Cootie Williams

COUNT BASIE

Another prolific pianist, inspired by the
Harlem school and Fats Waller in particular, Count Basie was born in Red Bank (NJ)
in 1904. He was taught piano by his mother
and toured in vaudeville in a vacancy he
took over from Fats Waller. In Kansas City
he joined the Bennie Moten Band, and after
that leader's death in 1935 Basie started his
own orchestra which bears some comparison
with Ellington's in that he was able to command similar loyalty from many sidemen.
On the other hand, his all-round musical
ability is less than Ellington's, his popularity
has been more variable, and he has made less
certain forays into uncharted territory. This,
though, merely shows that comparisons are
odious, and is not to underrate Basie's contribution to Jazz, his present popularity, and
unique drive.

Quentin Jackson

Sonny Payne

Count Basie

The Count Basie Orchestra 1969

Lester Young

Frank Wess

Freddie Green

The Count Basie Band and Count Basie (inset)

Chick Webb (inset) and his Orchestra, led here by Ella Fitzgerald, who took over after Webb's death

Ella Fitzgerald

CHICK WEBB

The first drummer ever to lead a Big Band, Chick Webb was born in Baltimore (Md) in 1902; he taught himself to play drums, worked the riverboats, and moved to New York in 1925. He formed his first band there the following year, and soon worked it up to Big Band line-up. By the early 1930s, he had built a tremendous reputation, especially among his fellow musicians, based on his unsurpassed drumming. In 1934 he discovered Ella Fitzgerald. From then on, his popularity grew but in 1938 he succumbed to tuberculosis and died the following year.

ELLA FITZGERALD

It was Ella Fitzgerald who carried on the Chick Webb band after its leader's death until 1942. She was born in Newport News (Va) in 1918, brought up in a New York orphanage, and discovered by Webb at a talent contest in 1934. He immediately recognized her worth, bought her a suitable wardrobe, and set her on the road to fame. After leaving the Webb Orchestra she be-

Jimmie Lunceford and his Orchestra – one of the most polished presentations of its time

Sy Oliver

Trummy Young

came a solo artiste, and from the mid-1940s she worked with the impresario Norman Grantz, who became her manager. She has often sung with Basie, Ellington and Oscar Peterson, yet there is still controversy as to whether or not she is a Jazz singer, since she has spent much time singing non-Jazz material on the night-club circuits.

BILLIE HOLIDAY

If there is argument about Ella Fitzgerald's classification, there is none about that of the legendary Lady Day. She was born in Baltimore (Md) in 1915; her father played guitar and banjo with Fletcher Henderson in the 1930s, during which years Billie was appearing in Harlem clubs. In 1933 she was discovered by John Hammond and made her first records with Benny Goodman, but Hammond was unable to persuade Goodman to take her on as a singer. However, within a couple of years she had laid the foundation of her international standing as a recording artiste with pianist Teddy Wilson, and later with tenor-player Lester Young, with whom she had a breath-taking musical rapport; she also made scores of other recordings and appearances with orchestras such as Duke Ellington's and Fletcher Henderson's. Billie Holiday's private life (which, in an artiste, is a part of public life) was increasingly fraught with battles against men, alcohol and drugs and with time the quality of her voice was variable, if not declining. She had served a prison sentence in 1948 for a narcotics offence, and was charged with another as she was dying in a New York hospital in 1959.

JIMMIE LUNCEFORD

In its heyday, Lunceford's orchestra was noted as the best colored Big Band of its time, and had the leader lived he might well be competing with Basie. Jimmie Lunceford was born in Fulton (Mo) in 1902 and studied music with Paul Whiteman's father; he was a multi-instrumentalist, though when he became a bandleader he played very little. His first band was formed in 1927 and rose to tremendous popularity in the mid-1930s. Much of its success stemmed from its chief arranger, trumpeter Sy Oliver, who created for it a style quite different from those of his contemporaries. Oliver, however, left Lunceford in 1939 and this, together with more changes in the line-up (there may be some connection), led to a decline in popularity of the Lunceford orchestra. It continued, however, until the death of its leader in 1947.

Billie Holiday

Spot the odd man out – James Stewart plays the part of Glenn Miller in *The Glenn Miller Story*, as an all-star jam session at Connie's Inn, Harlem, in 1928 is recreated in 1953. James Stewart, Trummy Young, Louis Armstrong, Cozy Cole, Gene Krupa, Barney Bigard, Arvel Shaw and Marty Napoleon

7/THE SWING ERA

All the orchestras we have met so far (with the exception of Paul Whiteman's) have been colored, and therefore 'expected' to play Jazz. Moreover, they all came into being in the 1920s. There was a parallel development among White orchestras which were 'expected' to play dance music, and this led to the Swing Era.

The word 'swing' has two musical meanings – a quality of music, or a type of music. The musical quality is an indefinable something which lifts the ordinary performance on to a higher plane; it is felt by musicians and audiences alike – everything is going right, the whole is greater than the sum of its parts, there is a rapport which defies description, the music swings.

Jelly Roll Morton's *Georgia Swing* dates from 1906 – perhaps he did give the word its musical meaning. However, a much more widely-known work is Ellington's *It Don't Mean A Thing If It Ain't Got That Swing* (1932), which clearly introduced Swing as something which it was essential to have, even if nobody knew exactly what it was. It was probably at about this time that the word Swing was adopted as an alternative to Jazz to describe the music of the Big Bands, and quickly spread. The British Broadcasting Corporation, for example, guardian and arbiter of taste, decided that to describe music as Swing was acceptable, whereas to describe the same music as Jazz was not.

In fact, nobody attempts to describe Swing except in terms of Fats Waller's alleged reply to a lady questioner with the same problem: 'If you gotta ask, you ain't got it.' This brings us back to Swing being a quality rather than a type of music, and I am drawn to the conclusion that Swing as something new was a mirage; it was applied to Jazz, especially Big Band Jazz, as soon as Benny Goodman was crowned King of Swing. A king must have a kingdom; what started as a jingly title led to the erroneous conclusion that he who played in the same style as Goodman must be playing Swing.

Now that it had a different name, many Jazz fans were able to declare that Swing was not Jazz, and that musicians who played it had reneged on their cultural heritage. Today, our longer historical perspective allows us to see that Swing was a form of Jazz played by Dance Bands of the 1930s, and it was intrinsically no better or worse than Jazz.

Pianist and composer Stan Kenton started to lead his own band in the early 1940s, and became known for his 'Progressive Jazz'

John Kirby's Orchestra – bassist John Kirby started on trombone, played with Henderson, Millinder and Webb until forming his own band from 1937 to the mid-1940s, by which time his popularity had waned. He died in 1952

GLEN GRAY'S CASA LOMA ORCHESTRA

Swing seems to have arisen from the activities of white orchestras ostensibly playing dance music, but wishing to play Jazz. In the late 1920s, there was a band of Canadians, the Orange Blossom Band, playing at the Casa Loma Hotel, Toronto. In 1929, the band moved to New York City, and became the Casa Loma Orchestra under the leadership of its alto saxophonist Glen Gray. The contribution of the Casa Loma Orchestra to Jazz lay in their introducing it into their repertoire of dance music – successfully. The Casa Loma Orchestra may therefore be looked upon as the first link in that chain of musical development which led to the Swing Era. Much of the success of this orchestra throughout the 1930s was due to the arrangements of Gene Gifford, who also arranged for Fletcher Henderson and others. Glen Gray, who was born at Roanoke (Ill) in 1906, retired in the mid-1950s, but he continued to gather musicians together to record under his name from time to time. He died in 1963, but his name has lived on in nostalgic recreations of his music.

Benny Goodman

Glen Gray and his famous Casa Loma Orchestra

Eddie Sauter

Jess Stacey

BENNY GOODMAN

Among the sidemen of Ben Pollack, the NORK drummer who went on to lead bands of his own from the mid-1920s (see Chapter 5), were many who were later to lead bands in the Swing Era, including Benny Goodman. Goodman was born in Chicago (Ill) in 1909 and studied the clarinet; he joined Ben Pollack at the end of 1926, but at the same time he recorded with his own

Benny Goodman and (inset) Buck Clayton

Peggy Lee, Roy Eldridge (left inset) and Gene Krupa (right inset)

group. He left Pollack in 1929, became a freelance, then formed his first Big Band in 1934, touring the States the following year.

This was not a very successful venture until the Band reached the West Coast. The audience at the Palomar Ballroom in Los Angeles knew what to expect from Goodman – they had heard his records – and he was thus not playing to those who expected to hear a dance band, but was preaching to the converted. It so happened that the date was being broadcast and Goodman's tumultuous reception was relayed from coast to coast. Almost by accident the Swing Era had begun – 21 August 1935 – and Goodman was crowned King of Swing. He went on to make films, hundreds of recordings, radio and TV shows, concerts at Carnegie Hall,

Glenn Miller

world tours, with groups large and small. Not the least of his contributions was bringing together Black and White musicians through his early trio and quartet, the latter with agile vibesman Lionel Hampton, pianist Teddy Wilson and drummer Gene Krupa.

He continues to work with groups of various sizes, and to embrace a much wider musical field than Jazz (or Swing) alone, having played the Classics; he commissions pieces from leading contemporary composers. A biographical film, *The Benny Goodman Story*, was made in 1955.

GLENN MILLER

Another biographical film, *The Glenn Miller Story*, was made in 1953. This, however, was less accurate than Benny Goodman's, since its hero had disappeared in 1944. Glenn Miller was born in Clarinda (Iowa) in 1904, and played trombone with Ben Pollack and others in the late 1920s onwards, until forming his own band in 1937. By the beginning of the war he was immensely popular for his unique 'sound' and presentation – the latter inspired by Jimmie Lunceford's Orchestra. He joined the army in 1942 and formed an orchestra to entertain the troops; in 1944 he was touring and broadcasting in Britain and at the end of that year was sent to France to entertain there. He took off in a light aircraft, which was lost without trace. But, tragic as this was, his sound was not lost; the orchestra lived on under other leaders, and its sound is also to be heard from reverent copyists.

THE
DORSEY BROTHERS

Jimmy Dorsey, reedsman, was born in Shenandoah (Pa) in 1904; his trombone-playing brother Tommy was born the following year. Their father was a music teacher who ran a brass band in which his sons played. Both went on to play with many well-known bands – including the Paul Whiteman Orchestra – from the mid-1920s until 1933, when they formed their own band. This was short-lived; the brothers disagreed violently and went their separate ways in 1935, each forming his own orchestra, each rising to fame in the Swing Era. In 1953 they came together again when Jimmy joined Tommy's orchestra, but the reconciliation had a brief future for Tommy died in 1956. Jimmy took over the leadership but himself died the following year. The trombone player Warren Covington carried on the Dorseys' name until 1961.

Jimmy Dorsey

Tommy Dorsey

Teddy Wilson

Bobby Hackett

Charlie Shavers

Buddy Rich

ARTIE SHAW

Since Benny Goodman had already taken the title 'King of Swing,' his rival Artie Shaw became 'King of the Clarinet.' Shaw was born in New York City in 1910 and learned saxes and clarinet, played with various groups; then retired from music for a year in 1934. The following year he created a stir by playing at a Swing concert with a string quartet – this must have been more of a novelty than a lasting attraction, for he formed a Big Band with strings, which failed. He therefore assembled a conventional Big Band, which was an immediate success and, since both leaders played clarinet, he inevitably became compared and contrasted with Benny Goodman. The pressures of his undoubted success led him to disband for a second time. But he re-formed bands of various sizes and compositions from time to time: one of the most successful names under which he played was Artie Shaw and his Gramercy Five. The same commercial pressures forced him to retire finally in 1955 – to Spain – a victim of his own personality and popularity.

LIONEL HAMPTON

The first Jazz vibesman, Lionel Hampton, born in Louisville (Ky) in 1913, started as a drummer. Although he led his own band at first, it was his membership of Benny Goodman's quartet which made him widely known, and enabled him to re-emerge as a successful leader of his own Big Band in 1940. Although Jazz purists would question the taste of some of his showmanship, not least his two-fingered piano-playing (à la vibes), nobody could fault his enthusiasm and his ability to inspire those who play with him.

Lionel Hampton

Artie Shaw and his Band in the film *Second Chorus*

Lionel Hampton

Woody Herman

Harry James

WOODY HERMAN

Reedsman Woody Herman was born in Milwaukee (Wisc) in 1913, and was a child prodigy, appearing in vaudeville as the Boy Wonder of the Clarinet at the age of nine; he also took up the alto sax at that age. After playing with various groups, he formed his first (successful) band in 1936. 'The Band that plays the Blues' was the billing – every-one needs a shout-line – although its scope was much wider than that. Three years later came the million-selling record *Woodchopper's Ball*, still highly popular. In 1943, Herman reorganized, dropped the specific 'Blues' title, and emerged with his First Herd. Since then, there have been countless Herds, and countless front-rank musicians have passed through them.

CHARLIE BARNET

Charlie Barnet was born in New York City in 1913. His parents were rich, and wanted their son to become a corporation lawyer: he wanted to be a Jazz reedsman, and won.

By the age of sixteen he was leading his own band, which played on transatlantic liners; from then until the mid-1960s he led a series of groups, but played little after that. His band of 1939–45 was one of the most popular of the Swing Era, but his name seems to be less well known nowadays than he deserves.

HARRY JAMES

Born into a circus family in Albany (Ga) in 1916, Harry James learnt to play the trumpet with his father, and joined Ben Pollack before he was twenty. Late in 1936, he started to play with Benny Goodman and in 1939 left to form his own group. It was then that he started to play sweet rather than hot, which led many people to forget his Jazz foundation. He retired from music at the beginning of the 1950s, but later returned to the scene, re-formed a band and toured Europe, playing in the Jazz idiom once again. He thus regained his stature as a Jazz musician, and has continued to play and tour, with great popularity, amongst a new public.

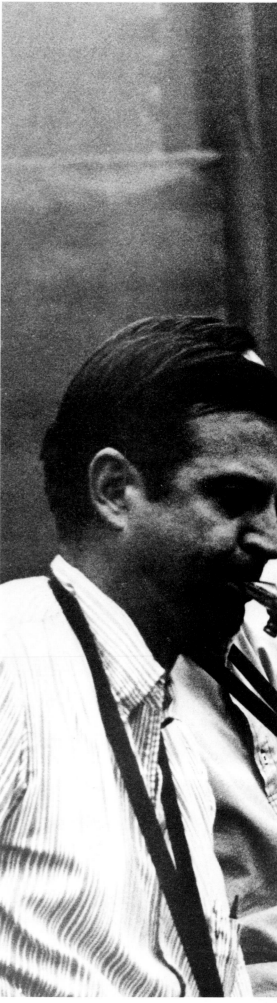

Down among the reeds – Charlie Barnet (3rd from left) on soprano sax, with Al Lasky, Willie Smith and Bob Jung

Bob Zurke – fine White Boogie

MORE BOOGIE WOOGIE

We saw in Chapter 4 that Boogie reached its height of popularity in the late 1930s, coincident with the Swing Era. One musical characteristic common to both Boogie and Swing is the riff, a musical figure repeated over and over again. The Boogie riff at its best varies from one chorus to the next, building up to a climax at the end of the piece, or dying away delicately and peacefully. By symbiosis, soon degenerating into parasitism, some Swing bands borrowed the Boogie form and, as suggested earlier, thus led it to the slaughter.

Others used the device more gracefully, for example, the Bob Crosby Band which enjoyed Bob Zurke's piano from 1936–39. Zurke is considered to be the greatest White exponent of Boogie at that time; born in Detroit (Mich) in 1910, he formed his own (unsuccessful) Big Band after leaving Crosby, and died in 1944, having spent his last few years as a night-club pianist.

Red Norvo – pioneer vibesman

Bill Harris

Eddie Safranski

Stan Kenton

WHAT HAPPENED TO SWING?

In this and the previous chapter we have seen the rise of the Big Band and the emergence of the Swing Era, a musical event which can be dated very accurately. Many of the most popular musicians of the Swing Era are still going strong, and we are now quite accustomed to sounds which were new and exciting some forty years ago, though this is not to say that present practitioners lack zest and excitement – just that their music has become absorbed into our culture.

Swing could be said to have divided into three particularly identifiable streams. The first comprises those who have remained in the forefront, balancing progress and popularity, playing a music of their own. The second comprises those who play what came to be called Mainstream Jazz – a mixed bag of idioms, swinging and easy on the ear. The third trades on nostalgia and recreates the sounds of the Swing Era, Glenn Miller's, as ever, being top favorite.

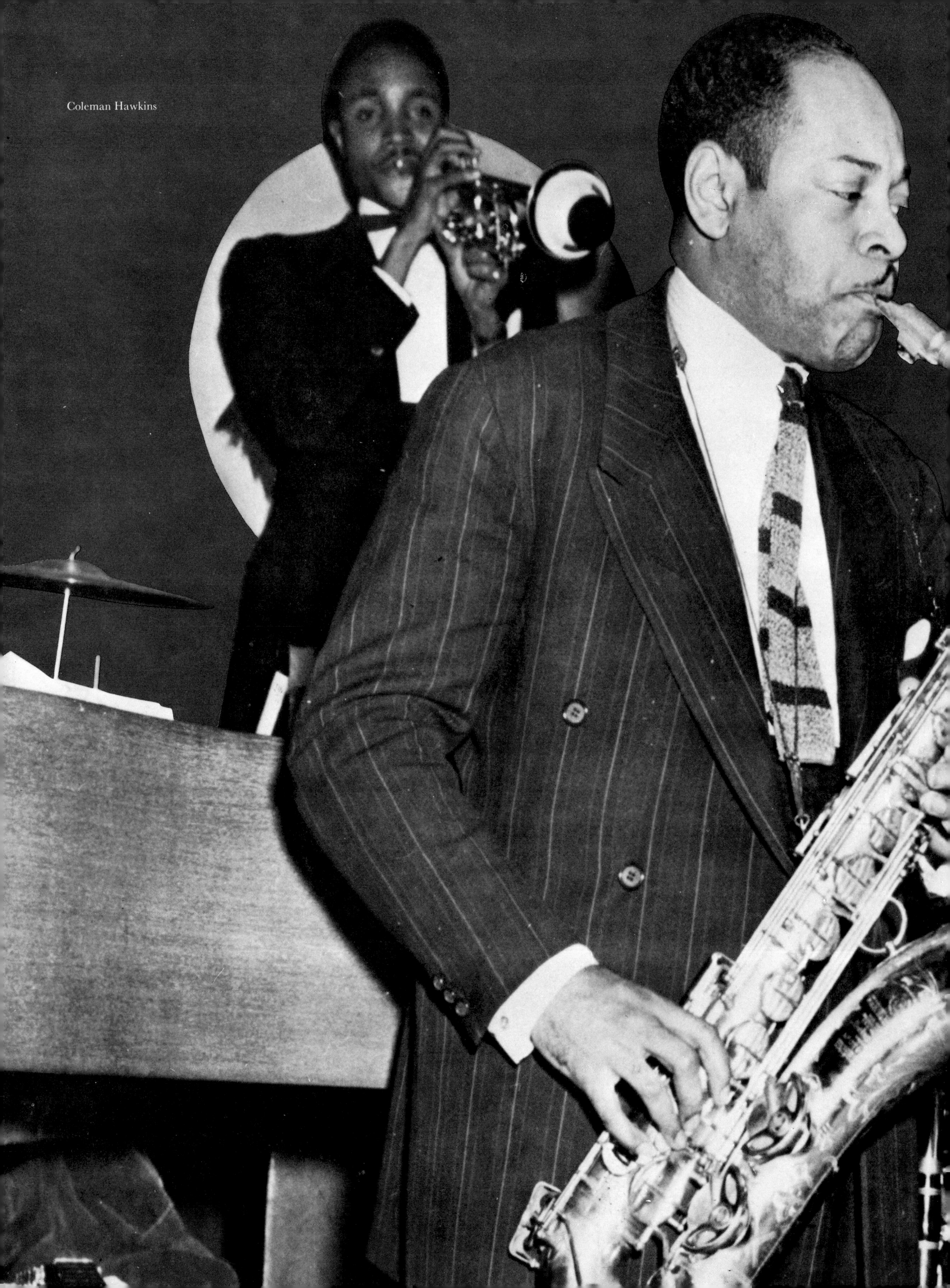
Coleman Hawkins

8/JAZZ IN THE 1940s

Although ten-year cycles are artificial periods, relating the development of Jazz to the decades of the century can help us to see its stages in historical perspective.

In the first decade, 1901–10, there is the emergence of New Orleans Jazz itself. In the second, riverboat and wartime activity took Jazz to points north, notably Chicago – and the ODJB recorded. In the third, Jazz gained its wider public through the proliferation of bands and recordings; this period also saw the rise of the Vaudeville Blues singers, and, toward its end, the Big Bands. In the fourth decade, as we have just seen, came the popularity of Boogie, and the Swing Era.

This brings us to 1940, the start of a decade in which Jazz took off in a variety of directions, some of which we have already discussed, others which we must now examine and which may even, for some purists, have left the world of Jazz altogether. It takes time for events to be seen in their proper perspectives, and it is more difficult when charting their recent progress to

Illinois Jacquet (b. 1922) set out as a soprano and alto player, but first came to prominence with his performance on tenor with Lionel Hampton's Orchestra in *Flying Home* in the early 1940s. His freak, extrovert playing started a new school of tenormen who perhaps overlooked the more lasting contribution to Jazz he had to offer when in thoughtful mood. Jacquet later returned to the other members of the sax family, and also introduced the bassoon into his armoury – a new Jazz diversion

state whether such progress is part of Jazz. Perhaps Jelly Roll Morton was wrong, or right only for his times, when he said: 'Jazz is to be played sweet, soft, plenty rhythm.' But if he *was* uttering a timeless truth, at least one, if not two or all of his criteria, may not apply to more recent music.

Race Music

In looking at Blues guitarists in Chapter 3, we saw that many of them survived into the 1950s and beyond, enjoying a wide popularity. In about 1950, the term Race Music became unacceptable for discriminatory reasons, and was replaced by Rhythm and Blues – R&B for short.

R&B was revitalized and rose to even greater popularity as a result of at least three factors. First, there was the vogue for discovering forgotten musicians – or those thought to be lost even if they were not – which brought forward many guitar players and, later, copyists. Second, the style, which was based on the 12-bar Blues sequence, owed something to the tail end of

Big Joe Turner (b. 1911), the Kansas City bartender turned Blues singer, who worked with pianist Pete Johnson in his native city until they explored the wider fields offered by the Boogie boom. His great shouting voice was accompanied by many other pianists, including Meade Lux Lewis, Joe Sullivan and Art Tatum. His fame and popularity emerged afresh with the development of R&B in the early 1950s – Turner produced the genuine article

the Boogie boom; Boogie, which had been inspired by Rural Blues guitarists in the first place, paid them back with interest. Third, the development of electronics allowed performers to make their sounds, which had earlier been quiet and intimate, fill a large hall.

In parallel with R&B arose the white analogue, a less thoughtful and more commercial and brash musical manifestation, also based on the 12-bar Blues sequence: Rock 'n' roll. Using the three-chord trick, anyone could do it (some better than others) and a new field was tilled and sown. From such seeds grew the Pop industry of today, a complex interplay among groups (from the Beatles downward), electronics developments, mass-marketing and market-creation techniques – a whole study in itself.

Renewal

R&B was a naturally growing branch of the already well-established Blues limb of the Jazz tree. Our next chapter will look at the developments in Jazz which created a movement which it is convenient to cover with the umbrella title Modern Jazz. But there is another movement of the 1940s to be considered which, seeking for a neutral name, I have styled Renewal.

It was in the 1940s that the old Jazz, respectable and nostalgic, began to find a new audience. This was due not only to the fact that it still had some-

Ray Charles (b. 1932) – blind musician and R&B, Gospel and Jazz singer, who has managed to employ showmanship without swamping authenticity

Coleman Hawkins (1904–69), the first great master of the tenor sax and one of Jazz's greatest solo virtuosi. His career lasted from the late 1920s until his death, during which time he toured extensively and made numerous recordings, not least with his fellow sax player and closest rival, Lester Young

Below right: Albert Nicholas (1900–73), another clarinettist who personified the New Orleans style, and played with everybody who was anybody. He is seen here with Britain's Andy Cooper on a UK tour in the mid-1960s

thing powerful to say, but also because audiences found in its familiarity a relaxation which was lacking in the emerging Modern Jazz. Thus many of the older Jazzmen, still active but perhaps past their primes, were sought out; often (but by no means always) their curiosity values masked their limited musicianship.

Two rival camps sprang up: the Traditionalists and the Revivalists. Looking back, the amount of heat generated between the two, considering that both were trying to achieve much the same end, may seem remarkable. The Traditionalists based their music on what they thought New Orleans Jazz should be: a steady beat on the bass drum; a loud, obtrusive 4-to-the-bar banjo; positively no piano or saxophone. The Revivalists based their music on what they thought of as the less restricted, more developed sound of the Chicago Jazz recordings of the 1920s. But if New Orleans Jazz developed into Chicago Jazz, so did the two styles merge as time went on to be called today, by all but the most fanatical, either Trad (for short), or Dixieland.

Although the audiences for Trad have waxed and waned since the original boom, there are still many musicians, both amateur and professional, who find great enjoyment and relaxation in playing it. Many of those who lived to give to, and benefit from, the Renewal have already appeared in our pages; two more were particularly identified with the movement.

BUNK JOHNSON

One of the most publicized Renewalists was the trumpeter (and cornettist) Bunk Johnson, born in New Orleans (La) in 1879. He was thus on site for the birth of Jazz, and claimed that he played with Buddy Bolden from time to time, a possibility denied by Louis Nelson, who actually did.

However, Johnson's career did not develop in the same way as other Jazzmen's; rather than playing with well-known bands in New Orleans and moving up-river, he moved in vaudeville circuits, and by the time he retired from the musical scene in the early 1930s – with neither trumpet nor teeth as the result of a dance-hall fight – was something of a legend. In 1937, he was sought out by the researchers Frederic Ramsey Jr and William Russell; five years later, they provided him with a new trumpet and a new set of teeth made by Sidney Bechet's brother, Leonard, and he became the center of the New Orleans revival with Lu Watters' Yerba Buena Jazz Band in San Francisco.

Bunk Johnson's early history, insofar as one can separate fact from fiction, seems to present him as a competent player who happened to be in the right place at the right time, rather than the great Jazz pioneer who taught Louis Armstrong. Whatever the case, Bunk made his mark before his death in 1949.

GEORGE LEWIS

George Lewis was the New Orleans clarinettist who survived for rediscovery at the appropriate time. He was born in 1900, taught himself to play the clarinet and from the mid-1910s until the Depression played with numerous bands, including those of Kid Ory and Buddy Petit.

In the 1930s he played less, but was ripe for the New Orleans revival in 1942. After his initial appearances with Bunk Johnson, Lewis formed his own band which toured extensively to mixed receptions. However, when he was in tune, he did produce the sound of the classic New Orleans clarinet comparable with that of any other practitioner. He died in his native city in 1968.

Although there are hundreds, if not thousands, of other musicians associated with the New Orleans revival, those who actually sparked it off are less numerous. Certainly Johnson and Lewis were of great importance; other musicians whom we have already met did not disappear from the scene to be rediscovered later; rather they adapted what they had to offer so that their capabilities met the commercial needs of the time. And they played to audiences whose interests were different from those of yore: instead of dancing and shouting, they sat in rows, wrapt. They had gone to listen to living legends – and it was sometimes difficult to separate the curiosity value from the product itself; one wondered not that it was done well, but that it was done at all. For those who enjoyed it, it was in powerful contrast to the other sounds now emerging, the like of which had not been heard before.

Bunk Johnson

George Lewis and British bandleader Mister Acker Bilk

9/MODERN JAZZ

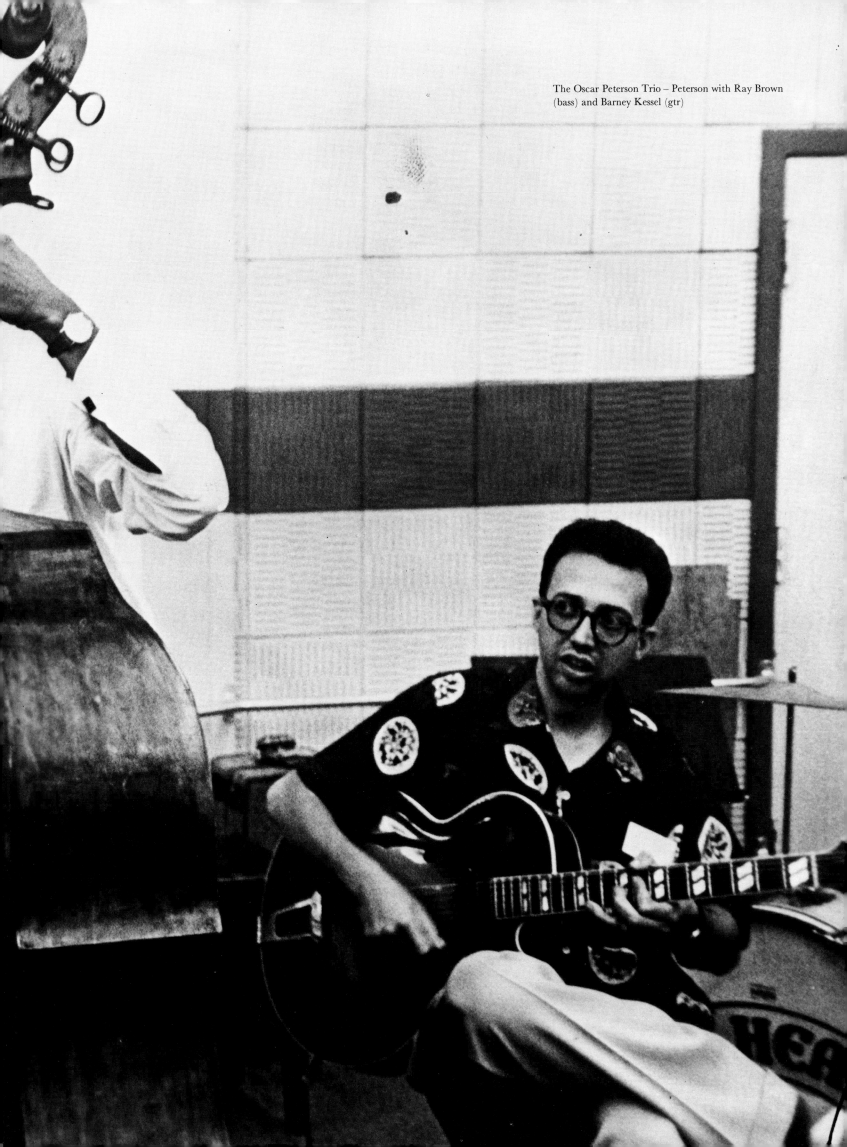

The Oscar Peterson Trio – Peterson with Ray Brown
(bass) and Barney Kessel (gtr)

Modern Jazz is a convenient term for the developmental stream which we will now examine, rather than a reference to the times in which it was, or is, played. Put simply, the characteristic of Modern Jazz is to modify – to lose, even – the rhythms, harmonies and melodies of the music we have discussed so far. Rhythmically, Modern Jazz departs from the solid beat; thus, for a start, the roles of the low and high frequencies in the drum-kit are reversed, the cymbals maintaining a rhythm while the bass drum punctuates it. Harmonically, more ambitious chords are used, often to form new progressions from one point in a familiar sequence to another. Melodically, the emphasis may shift from a singable tune to a series of notes of shorter durations, built on the modified chord progressions.

Not that all these modifications were introduced at once in fully-fledged form, but the beginning of Modern Jazz – Rebop, Bebop or just Bop – was a sufficiently radical departure from conventional thinking at the beginning of the 1940s to produce hostile audiences and misunderstood musicians. The exponents of the new styles may seem to have sprung more from the schools of musical training, and may seem to rely more on technical virtuosity than on the musicianship of their earlier colleagues. Looking back, however, we can make the same observations about some of their earlier colleagues. As always, time alone will tell which musicians have made a significant contribution to Jazz; meanwhile, critics are sharply divided in their opinions on the worth of the work of practising musicians who are trying to push forward the frontiers of their art.

Rahsaan Roland Kirk (1936–77), visionary and multi-instrumentalist, a one-man Jazz band who played remarkable music even after a stroke which paralyzed his right arm in 1976

Thelonious Monk – enigmatic pianist

Max Roach, Charlie Parker and Kenny Clarke at a Paris Jazz Festival in 1949

Dizzy Gillespie

DIZZY GILLESPIE

Dizzy Gillespie was born in Cheraw (SC) in 1917, and learnt to play several instruments before settling for the trumpet. He was first influenced by Roy Eldridge (six years his senior) whom he replaced in Teddy Hill's Band in 1937, and with which he toured Europe. This band, and its leader's subsequent tenure at Minton's Play House (meeting place of Bop musicians, if not the very womb of Bop), are Hill's chief claims to fame as an architect of the new music. Gillespie joined Cab Calloway in 1939, and it is at about this time that the elements of Bop become apparent in his style. He moved from band to band (particularly notable: Billy Eckstine and Earl Hines) until Bop emerged in the mid-1940s, and with it the name of Dizzy Gillespie. He then formed bands of his own and took the new music on tour, but was always forced to include some more familiar – and thus understandable – music in his programs. Nowadays, much early Bop is itself so familiar as to pass unnoticed.

As Armstrong had said something new in the 1920s, so did Gillespie in the 1940s. Perhaps the high spot of his recognition came in 1956 when the US government sent him on the first subsidized goodwill tour as an ambassador of Jazz. Since then, he has received many honors in recognition of his contribution to music. One of the articulate modern school, he has shared and developed his music with students at seminars, a far cry from some of the older musicians whose attitude often seems to have been to prevent copyists at all costs.

Billy Eckstine, singer and bandleader, nursed Bop talent

Sarah Vaughan, pioneer Bop singer with phenomenal voice

CHARLIE PARKER

Charlie Parker's career was tragically short. He was born in Kansas City (Kan) in 1920, and was brought up in the other Kansas City (Mo). His mother bought him an alto saxophone when he was eleven; four years later, he had left school and started his musical career somewhat disastrously, when he sat in with a local band, played very badly and was forcibly ejected. Far from being permanently discouraged, he vowed that he would go away, learn all he could, and return to redeem his reputation. Few people could have done such a thing as magnificently as Parker did; he not only mastered his instrument, he became a first-rate composer and arranger and played an essential part in the forging of Bop. He met Dizzy Gillespie in the early 1940s: both men had been thinking musically along the same lines – as had countless others less well known. But by 1946

Parker, who had been a drug addict since leaving school, was in bad health, exacerbated by adverse criticism of his music. He went into Camarillo State Hospital to be cured; after six months he was released and continued to tour and play until the early 1950s when his health deteriorated again; he died in 1955.

That Bop was 'invented' by Gillespie and Parker is widely believed, but patently untrue. Development of a style is not a calculated look at what exists so that the next step can be taken coolly and logically, neither is it a desire to make some artistically shocking gesture for the sake of being different. If there is a particular artistic climate, a number of people in different places will be affected by it, and it is clear that many thinking along the same lines will eventually meet and reinforce one another's ideas.

Kenny Clarke

Charlie Parker in 1951

KENNY CLARKE

We touched earlier on the interchange of the roles of the bass drum and the cymbal in Bop. Kenny Clarke, born into a musical family in Pittsburgh (Pa) in 1914, was one of the pioneers of this style. He was a multi-instrumentalist who played with Roy Eld-

OSCAR PETTIFORD

The original Bop bassist was Oscar Pettiford, born in Okmulgee (Okla) in 1922 into a large musical family. He started to learn the piano at the age of eleven, and the bass at fourteen. He toured with the family band (parents and eleven Pettiford children) until 1941. Two years later, he was co-leader with Dizzy Gillespie of an early Bop group. Subsequently, apart from leading his own band, he spent periods with Duke Ellington and Woody Herman until settling in Europe in the late 1950s, but his health suddenly deteriorated and he died in Copenhagen in 1960.

BUD POWELL

The pianist of Bop was Bud Powell, born in New York City in 1924, also into a musical family. He brought an extraordinary energy to the keyboard which was admired not only by his young, emulating followers, but also by his seniors. Such dynamism takes its toll; from the mid-1940s, his mental health was uncertain. He worked in France from 1959–64, where he deteriorated physically as well, and when he returned to the US he did little more work and died in 1966.

Bud Powell

Oscar Pettiford

ridge – the Gillespie connection – and the Teddy Hill Band (after Gillespie had left). He and Gillespie later joined forces, which was not surprising, considering their common influences. Clarke later became one of the founder-members of the Modern Jazz Quartet, with whom he stayed for three years before emigrating to France, where he has spent most of his time since.

THELONIOUS MONK

Another pianist, extraordinary in a different way from Bud Powell, is Thelonious Monk. He was born in Rocky Mount (NC) in 1917; his family moved to New York City, and in time Monk found himself in the group which was shaping Bop. Yet until the late 1950s, he remained in comparative obscurity, perhaps because he is a musicians' musician, highly regarded by (some of) his fellows and misunderstood by most other people. Gradually, this enigmatic and eccentric man gained a following and in 1971–72 he toured with Dizzy Gillespie and others, playing as The Giants of Jazz. Although his appearances seem to have been curtailed somewhat, both by inclination and by ill health, he continues to inspire rising generations of young pianists.

Thelonious Monk

MJQ

One of the longest-lived and widely known modern groups was the Modern Jazz Quartet which existed from 1952 until 1974. The first MJQ sprang from the Dizzy Gillespie Orchestra and comprised the pianist John Lewis, doyen of modern vibesmen Milt Jackson, drummer Kenny Clarke and bassist Ray Brown. Clarke and Brown were replaced by Connie Kay and Percy Heath a year or so after the formation of the MJQ; thereafter, the group was stable. The fact that the MJQ was widely recognized outside Jazz circles, highly popular, and so long-lived, says as much for it as for its music. Those who find brass and reeds strident – as many do – will describe the MJQ as restful, showing that it's not what you play, but the way that you play it.

Thelonious Monk

MJQ

John Lewis

Milt Jackson

BUDDY DE FRANCO

Born in Camden (NJ) in 1923, de Franco was the only Bop clarinettist of note, leading his own Big Band in 1951 and, later, a quartet. From 1966–74 he became leader of the Glenn Miller Orchestra with which he toured the world; since then he has turned his energies toward writing and arranging.

JAY JAY JOHNSON

The Bop trombonist was Jay Jay Johnson, born in Indianapolis (Ind) in 1924. He started studying the piano but changed to the trombone at the age of fourteen, and acquired a facility on the slide which until then had been attainable only by valves. In spite of his formidable technique and his playing with top men – Basie, Gillespie, Herman – he was unable to make a living from music, and retired for a couple of years in the summer of 1952. He then joined the Danish-born trombonist Kai Winding to form the Jay and Kay Quintet. Toward the end of the 1950s, Johnson turned more towards composing and arranging until today he is known more widely in that role than as a performer.

CHARLIE CHRISTIAN

The pioneer Bop guitarist was Charlie Christian, born in Dallas (Texas) in 1919. He joined Benny Goodman in 1939; his significant contribution was the use of the electric guitar on which he played virtuoso single-string solos – a technique so common now as to pass unnoticed, but unheard of before Christian. While with Goodman, he fell in with the Boppers at Minton's; apart from a new sound, which must have pleased them, he may even have invented the word Bebop. But he had precious little time in which to contribute; he contracted tuberculosis in 1941, and died early the following year.

AFTER BOP

Bop was but the beginning of a new stream of Jazz which seemed to be more for musicians than for audiences, until the audiences became accustomed to it. This stream is analogous to Modern Art of the sort where the artist wishes to express himself but finds that being misunderstood by the public is almost mandatory. But the public does, eventually, become accustomed to it, by which time, of course, the pioneer artists are well into the next phase but two, and the copyists of their previous styles are well under way.

The players discussed previously were selected from those who founded and popularized the Modern Jazz stream; there were of course scores of others. My final selection moves through the realms of Hard Bop, Cool Jazz, Free Jazz, and into uncharted territories. They are presented according to their dates of birth, on the assumption that age may at least have been some determining factor on the point at which they entered the world of Jazz, and since we have to stop somewhere, I have taken my closing year of birth as 1930. However, before we move into these uncharted territories, we should consider broadly what these musicians were trying to do.

Bop tried to break away from Jazz conventions and, in its time, succeeded. It altered the voicing of rhythm, without

Buddy de Franco

Charlie Christian

Jay Jay Johnson

necessarily making it more complex than Jazz had known before. It experimented with new harmonies, which at first sounded 'wrong.' It escaped from simple chord sequences, yet still confined itself within more complex ones. In a comparatively short time, its sounds became familiar – so what could Jazz do next?

It exploited its rhythmic element. The drums, which had already broken away from their conventional task of laying down a steady beat, became a front-line instrument, and thus took on a very new role. At the same time, the piano was treated more as a percussion instrument so that instead of the accustomed melodic exchanges between, say, trumpet and sax, we now find rhythmic exchanges between drums and piano.

The pioneer group was named, appropriately enough, the Jazz Messengers, and was formed in 1954 by drummer Art Blakey and pianist Horace Silver – what they played came to be known as Hard Bop. Silver left Blakey in 1956 to form his own group, and developed his brand of Hard Bop still further by allowing the influence of Negro church music to act upon it: the result was named Funky or Soul Jazz. According to how you look at it, this was either a success or a disaster because it became popular. Certainly, popularity spells success, but equally, if your audience immediately appreciates what you are doing, it may indicate that you are not doing anything new enough.

As a contrast to the driving force of Hard Bop we find Cool Jazz. The proponent of this style was trumpeter (and flügelhorn player) Miles Davis, and his early experiments, which were too advanced to be commercially successful, included the distant voice of the French horn and the return of the tuba in a new role. The harmonic writing was such that the fullest sound could be produced with the fewest possible instruments; later, for example, the famed Gerry Mulligan Quartet played without a piano. Cool Jazz was not developed as a deliberate contrast to Hard Bop; Miles Davis's advanced recordings *The Birth of the Cool* were made in 1949, five years before the formation of the Jazz Messengers.

In Free, or Avant-Garde, Jazz, the music appears to have met developments in the non-Jazz world head on, and such words as 'atonality' and 'incoherence' are bandied about, according to the views of the people who are bandying. Such music is related not only to the natural experimental development of the art, but also to the expression of political ideas, which has in turn led to misunderstanding and suppression. One cannot help feeling that this is not really what art is supposed to be for.

Art Blakey

GIL EVANS

One of the foremost composer/arrangers of the period was Gil Evans, born in Toronto in 1912. He led his own band through most of the 1930s in Stockton (Cal); and when it was taken over, he continued as its arranger. He spent most of the 1940s with the Claude Thornhill Orchestra, arranging in new and exciting ways (Thornhill used French horns) which, however, went almost entirely unnoticed. As the 1950s dawned, Evans moved into Cool Jazz with the controversial Miles Davis, Gerry Mulligan and others. He also started to play the piano and tour, which he has continued through the 1960s and 1970s, at the same time building up a formidable range of compositions, including much commissioned music.

PETE RUGOLO

Born in Sicily in 1915, Pete Rugolo moved to the US in about 1920 and studied music, later under Darius Milhaud; he played Jazz piano from his teens. His career turned toward composing and arranging – he was responsible for the sound of the Stan Kenton Orchestra in the second half of the 1940s. Since then, he has devoted himself almost entirely to composing and directing for record companies, films and TV.

ART BLAKEY

Art Blakey, born in Pittsburgh (Pa) in 1919, is in the tradition of Jazz drummers who are also leaders, having formed his first Jazz Messengers in the mid-1950s, purveyors of Hard Bop. Blakey first played with Fletcher Henderson in 1939 and then, after various moves, worked with Billy Eckstine during the existence of the latter's orchestra – that cradle of Bop. Blakey drives himself, and his colleagues, to the limit, giving rise to great excitement for all who can stand the pace.

LENNIE TRISTANO

Born in Chicago (Ill) in 1919, this blind pianist studied music and played in public from an early age. He moved to New York City in the mid-1940s, and there founded his Cool school of Jazz, putting his experimental ideas into practice and opening a music school in 1951. From then on, he appeared infrequently in public, and made very few recordings, but his ideas have been widely promulgated through his pupils and his writings. He died in 1978.

Dave Brubeck

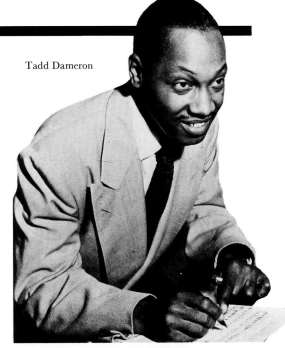

Tadd Dameron

TADD DAMERON

A short-lived but essential contributor to Bop was the composer/arranger and pianist Tadd Dameron, born in Cleveland (Ohio) in 1917. His association with the Dizzy Gillespie Orchestra in the mid-1940s made him the pioneer Big Band Bop arranger. Toward the end of the 1960s, he was imprisoned for a drugs offence, but emerged to write again before ill health overtook him and he finally succumbed to cancer in 1965.

DAVE BRUBECK

An important and widely-known pianist and composer, Dave Brubeck was born into a musical family in Concord (Calif) in 1920. He studied music from an early age, through college, and with Milhaud and Schoenberg. As well as this study, he played Jazz from his early teens and at the beginning of the 1950s formed his Quartet which became world famous through its recordings and tours. Until the mid-1960s, the Dave Brubeck Quartet featured the alto player Paul Desmond; at that time, however, Desmond seems to have felt that the directions of Modern Jazz did not suit him; he left, and has kept a low profile since. Desmond was to some extent the Jazz influence in the Quartet: Brubeck himself tended toward a musicians' music which left many critics uncertain of their reactions. After Desmond's departure, Brubeck's new Quartet featured the baritone player Gerry Mulligan. Brubeck has three musical sons, which enables the family to maintain its own Quartet. Not surprisingly, he has also devoted himself a good deal to composing, and has moved more and more toward the concert platform in recent years.

FATS NAVARRO

Trumpeter Fats Navarro was one of the foremost musical originators of his time and, had he lived, it seems clear that he would be ranked with, and as widely known as, Dizzy Gillespie. Navarro was born in Key West (Fla) in 1923, learned the piano and later the trumpet, and was of such caliber that he was able to succeed Dizzy Gillespie, on Gillespie's recommendation, in Billy Eckstine's Band in the mid-1940s. After that, he worked with Illinois Jacquet, Lionel Hampton and Coleman Hawkins and, toward the end of the 1940s, with Tadd Dameron. But drugs and TB took their toll and he died in 1950.

SONNY STITT

Born in Boston (Mass) in 1924 into a musical family – his father was a professor of music and his brother a concert pianist – Sonny Stitt started on the piano and then studied reeds, especially tenor and alto saxes. He developed his Bop style before meeting Charlie Parker, and it must have been somewhat galling to Stitt (if not to Parker) for the two to find that they had arrived at the same musical point independently. Stitt first came to the fore as an original voice with Dizzy Gillespie in the mid-1940s. He went on to record prolifically and tour extensively, more recently with The Giants of Jazz.

CHARLES MINGUS

Best known as a bassist, composer and truly inspiring leader, Charles Mingus was born in Nogales (Ariz) in 1922, and studied a number of instruments before taking up the bass. In the early 1940s, he played with a number of bands, notably those of Louis Armstrong, Kid Ory and Lionel Hampton, with the last of which he established himself as one of the foremost exponents of Bop. Before he became a composer in the mid-1950s, Mingus played with many other pioneers including Charlie Parker and Bud Powell. Some of his compositions were written, but more often he directed from the keyboard, suiting the development of his ideas to the musicians he had at the time, and giving rise to some remarkably exciting performances. Such a driving leader was not always easy to get on with, and he had frequent disagreements with both musicians and management. Ill health contributed to his semi-retirement in the mid-1960s, but he returned to the scene in the 1970s and made two European tours. He died in 1979.

Sonny Stitt

JOHN COLTRANE

John Coltrane, a multi-instrumentalist born in Hamlet (NC) in 1926, played with a number of the foremost modernists from the end of the 1940s: Dizzy Gillespie, Johnny Hodges, Earl Bostic, Miles Davis. In his search for a new direction, he experimented with Indian music in the early 1960s, which led him to a modal approach and in turn to act as an inspiration to his younger followers, but his health deteriorated and he died in 1967.

Left: John Coltrane   Charles Mingus

Miles Davis

MILES DAVIS

Trumpeter Miles Davis was born in Alton (Ill) in 1926, and took up his instrument at the age of thirteen. At eighteen, he played in Billy Eckstine's Orchestra with Dizzy Gillespie and Charlie Parker, and was soon playing with Parker. In 1948 he studied with Gil Evans, and then formed a band with Lee Konitz and Gerry Mulligan which played a Cool Jazz so far ahead of its time that the band lasted but two weeks. In the mid-1950s his quintet with John Coltrane pioneered another new direction, but no sooner had he established that than he started to work with young unknowns whom he discovered and developed. Although a critic of those who were further out than he, Davis himself moved toward the use of electronic instruments and effects, and some critics believe that he had said all that he had to say in Jazz by the end of the 1960s, which was plenty.

OSCAR PETERSON

Through a combination of his musical ability, articulate personality, and good management, Oscar Peterson has won an enormous audience both within the world of Jazz and without it, which has led to unwarranted criticism of his integrity. Peterson was born in Montreal in 1925 and learned the piano from the age of six: in his early teens he won a talent contest and a regular local radio spot. He was twenty-five before he left Canada to make an outstanding debut at Carnegie Hall, the start of his rise to international fame. He very soon started to work with a trio, at first bass and guitar, later guitar replaced by drums. But he has also

Oscar Peterson

Right: Max Roach

worked widely as a soloist, toured with Ella Fitzgerald, and made many outstanding duo recordings with other artists.

MAX ROACH

One of the greatest drummers of Modern Jazz, Max Roach, was born in New York City in 1925, and was early inspired by Kenny Clarke, whose innovations he developed, and continues to develop. From the mid-1940s he played with all the greats of Bop and its descendants and, in 1954, formed his own quintet which lasted until trumpeter Clifford Brown and pianist Richie Powell – Bud's brother, and arranger for the quintet – were killed in a car crash. After this setback, it took him some time to reorganize his group, and in the 1960s he fell from favor by introducing some campaigning for racial equality into his compositions. In the 1970s he came to the fore again in new roles, first with the formation of a group of percussion instruments; second as a teacher – in 1972 he became Professor of Music in the University of Massachusetts.

STAN GETZ

Another setter of the Cool Jazz scene was tenorman Stan Getz, born in Philadelphia (Pa) in 1927. In the 1940s, he was playing with Jack Teagarden, Stan Kenton, Benny Goodman and a Woody Herman Herd. Since the 1950s, he has led his own groups, and toured and lived abroad extensively. After his contribution to Cool Jazz, he was largely responsible for the Bossa Nova craze in the early 1960s, which led him further away from his Jazz experiments. Some critics rank Getz as one of the top tenormen of Jazz.

Stan Getz

GERRY MULLIGAN

Composer, arranger, baritone saxophonist and sometimes pianist Gerry Mulligan was born in New York City in 1927, and played with many of the groups we have already met until the end of 1952. Then in California, he conceived a group without a piano, which would give it greater freedom, and with trumpeter Chet Baker the Cool, West Coast, Gerry Mulligan Quartet was born. The Quartet lived on with various changes of personnel and voices, but its leader continued to work with other groups as well. His contribution seems to embrace the whole of the history of Jazz, while remaining individually modern.

HORACE SILVER

Pianist and composer Horace Silver, born in Norwalk (Conn) in 1928, was first inspired by Bud Powell. In the early 1950s, he played with Stan Getz, and was co-founder of Art Blakey's Jazz Messengers; he then formed his own quintet, and developed from Hard Bop to the foundations of the Soul and Funky schools, with Latin-American influences. More recently, he has become increasingly widely known as a songwriter, and has toured the world in the last decade.

Zoot Sims (b. 1925), versatile reedsman who has played up front with Benny Goodman, Woody Herman, Stan Kenton and Gerry Mulligan: consistent and swinging

Gerry Mulligan

Horace Silver

SONNY ROLLINS

Sonny Rollins was born in New York City in 1929 and, though he was exposed to a musical environment from an early age, came to decide upon music as a possible career comparatively late. It was not until the late 1940s that he started to play tenor with the Bopmen, Art Blakey, later Bud Powell and Miles Davis, later still Max Roach. In 1957 he started to lead his own groups, and soon became bracketed with Stan Getz as a top tenorman. However, he retired from 1959 to 1961 to practise and develop his ideas; then returned to the scene with new vigor to experiment with different presentations – which met with the well-known division of the critics until his ventures came into some musical perspective. He also toured widely until retiring again from 1968 to 1971 for another self-appraisal and self-seeking, which included Eastern mystical studies. Once again he returned renewed to compose and tour, playing to an even better understanding by audiences and critics.

Sonny Rollins

Ornette Coleman

ORNETTE COLEMAN

Multi-instrumentalist Ornette Coleman was born in Fort Worth (Texas) in 1930, taught himself alto, then tenor, and sax, and was playing R&B around 1950. During that decade he went on to study music part time and emerged with the new concept of Free Jazz: a form in which all conventional pre-planning is apparently cast aside. This gave rise to sharp controversy among both musicians and critics as to whether at one extreme nothing whatever musical was being said; at the other that the very freedom of the new music made it (paradoxically) similar to the old. The central view was that musical frontiers were indeed being pushed forward. Coleman continued to experiment, to develop his compositions and to inspire followers; as with Sonny Rollins his ideas have now found acceptance among many – there is, perhaps, more resistance from musicians than from an open-minded public.

10/THE INTERNATIONAL SCENE

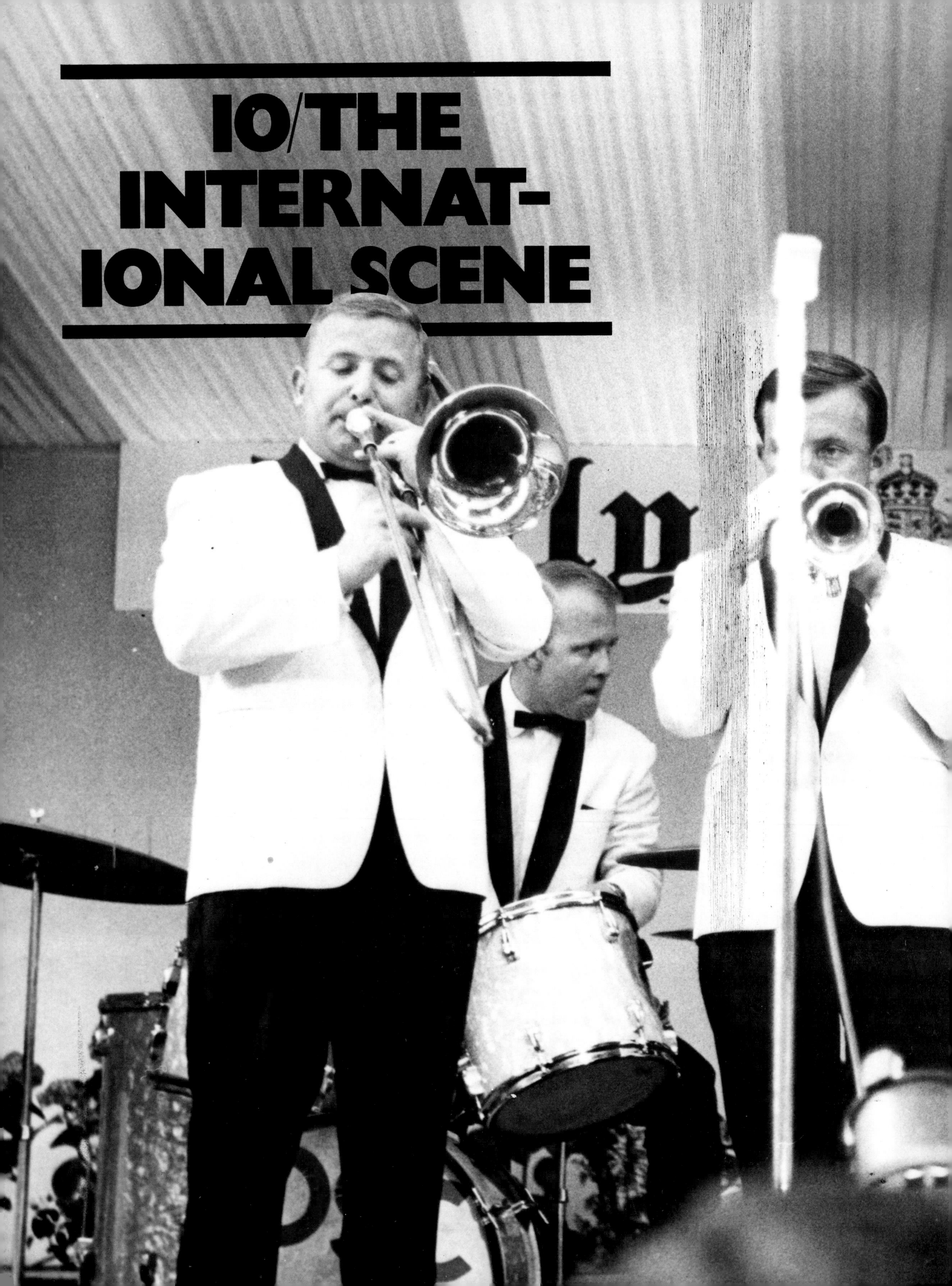

The Dutch Swing College Band on UK tour

Jazz is now a truly international music. Everywhere there are festivals, tours, interchanges of musicians and recordings, radio and television broadcasts. It has moved a long way since the visit of the ODJB to Britain 60 years ago: Jazz is not a suspect curiosity, it is a way of life.

Although I would hardly suggest that Jazz sprang fully armed out of America – for it had a long way to go in 1919 and is by no means at the end of its journey – its roots at that time were less well understood. Outside America, it was not surrounded with the same political and social taboos, and thus it was set fair to be more readily accepted as an art form once the original shock had abated. Between the wars, Jazz began to develop a life of its own in most parts of the globe according to the availability of films, records, indigenous or visiting musicians, and the attitudes of the management of broadcasting companies. Jazz had a message which touched the many who were open to receive it.

Perhaps it is no coincidence that an upsurge of interest in Jazz on the east side of the Atlantic coincided with the lifting of the pall of uncertainty and aggression when the Second World War ended. If one example be needed, consider the Dutch Swing College Band founded by clarinettist Peter Schilperoort in 1945 on the day of liberation. And that is just one example of what happened in Europe; we will return to others shortly.

Elsewhere in the world, we find that countries on the far side of the globe are no less active. Australia and New Zealand in the Southern Hemisphere have their worlds of Jazz. In the Northern Hemisphere, one of the greatest surprises, even in a rapidly Westernizing country, is the tremendous interest in Jazz in Japan, and the production by that country of a comparatively large number of outstanding musicians. Two major areas which seem more

The Dutch Swing College Band

musically isolated than the rest are China and India. Although they have strong musical cultures of their own, this in itself is not a bar to the development of Jazz, as Japan has shown, but there are of course strong political influences which differ for the three countries. Of late there has been some interchange of musical ideas with India, often bound up with increasing Western interest in mysticism. It will be interesting to see what musical developments the new entente with China inspires.

The post-war relief from tension mentioned earlier was no less great after the First World War, when the ODJB visited Britain, and it paved the way not only for further visits of American musicians purveying widely differing sounds under the name of Jazz, but also for a thriving British industry. At that time there was no clear idea in the public mind of exactly what Jazz was – perhaps this is still the case but to a lesser extent; doubtless a proportion of the public suffers from the same confusion in America today.

In 1923, the Paul Whiteman Orchestra visited the UK and, whatever the status of the music he played; Whiteman certainly helped to spread the interest in it. Far removed from Whiteman's symphonic syncopations was the music of the Mound City Blue Blowers, led by the kazoo-playing Red McKenzie, who visited in 1925. No sooner had this sound been assimilated, when Whiteman returned for a tour of London and the Provinces with a 27-piece orchestra; but by this time there was a growing understanding of the differences between Whiteman's music and Jazz.

That same year – 1926 – pianist Fred Elizalde formed his Quinquaginta Ramblers in Cambridge (England), and went on to import a number of top American musicians to play at London's Savoy Hotel in 1928 before returning to his native Spain to study music. Elizalde's Jazz successor was

Fred Elizalde's music – the leader is seated on the left

bassist Spike Hughes who, after leaving school in Cambridge, became the foremost name in British Jazz of his time, and widely known through his recordings for the Decca company (Spike Hughes and his Decca-dents) before moving to New York City in 1933, thus reversing the musical trend.

American musicians continued to visit – Louis Armstrong first came in 1933, Duke Ellington the same year, followed by violinist Joe Venuti, pianist Fats Waller and many others. More often than not, their appearances were at the now-defunct music halls throughout the country – such was the status of Jazz that they gave music hall (i.e. vaudeville) turns rather than concerts.

Then in 1935 came a disagreement between the Musicians' Union and the American Federation of Musicians which effectively stopped the British public from hearing live American musicians for some twenty years. American Jazz was available on record, via the British Broadcasting Corporation, in a few films, but if you wanted to hear it in the flesh you had to go abroad for it. Meanwhile, British Jazz developed through the dance orchestras, a notable advance being the employment of Benny Carter to arrange for the BBC in 1936; neither must we overlook the contribution of individuals such as George Chisholm, still going strong as one of the foremost Jazz trombonists.

Above: Benny Carter

Left: An international gathering – standing: Diz Disley (gtr), Beryl Bryden (sgr), George Chisholm (tmb); seated: Stephane Grappelli (vln) and Alex Welsh (tpt)

In the 1940s, there was a growing interest in Jazz in Britain; a new generation of people were discovering it for themselves, and this story was repeating itself elsewhere in the world. The singer and entertainer, George Melly, sums it up in his autobiographical volume *Owning Up*. Writing of his schooldays at Stowe:

'One summer evening a friend of mine called Guy Neal, whose opinion I respected, asked me to come and hear a record, it was called "Eccentric" and was by Muggsy Spanier. Guy explained that the three front-line instruments, trumpet, clarinet and trombone, were all playing different tunes and yet they all fitted together. We listened over and over again until it was dark. I walked across Cobham Court to my dormitory a convert.

Later that term I was passing an open study window and heard the most beautiful sound in the world. It was Louis Armstrong playing "Drop that Sack." I didn't know the boy who owned it, but I knocked on his door and asked if he would play it me again. I discovered that throughout the school there were little cells of jazz lovers. Slowly I learnt something

George Melly (seated) with John Chilton's Feetwarmers – Chuck Smith (dms), Stan Greig (pno), Barry Dillon (bass) and John Chilton (tpt)

Left: Humphrey Lyttelton (inset) and Humph with Australian pianist and bandleader Graeme Bell

about the music and its history, most of it inaccurate, all of it romantic. I heard my first Bessie Smith record. It was "Gimme a Pig-foot and a Bottle of Beer."

All over wartime Britain, at every class level the same thing was happening. . . . Suddenly, as if by some form of spontaneous combustion, the music exploded in all our heads.'

And so it was. A little later, I experienced the same excitement myself, organized record sessions at school, and was amazed to find how many enthusiastic collectors there were. Some of us got together and started to play ourselves; the same thing was happening up and down the country and during the 1950s a host of amateur musicians of all sorts was to appear as if from nowhere.

In 1943, at The Red Barn, a pub in Barnehurst, Kent, pianist George Webb's Dixielanders started to play to a growing public and a new phase in British Jazz was under way. The pioneering Dixielanders – who offered Jazz in the style of King Oliver – broke up three years later, but they had launched the now internationally-famous Humphrey Lyttelton, and Canadian-born clarinettist Wally Fawkes. The other trumpeter of this Oliver-inspired group was Owen Bryce who now, with his pianist-wife Iris, devotes much time teaching Jazz, when not exploring the inland waterways system in his floating home, narrowboat *Bix*.

The next landmark was the visit of the Graeme Bell Jazz Band from Australia. Bearing out our theory of the spontaneous generation of Jazz-bands, Graeme Bell had formed his in Melbourne in 1943, and had been selected to visit the Prague Youth Festival in Czechoslovakia in 1947. Having been well received there, they decided to pop over to tour England. They started quietly and ended tumultuously; apart from anything else, they encouraged happy jiving as opposed to wrapt listening.

In 1949, trumpeter Ken Colyer formed what was to become the Crane River Jazz Band. A perfectionist, Colyer visited New Orleans to study the

Ottilie Patterson – amazing singer with Chris Barber's Band and, below right, Ken Colyer

Chris Barber

Mister Acker Bilk

The Crane River Jazz Band – Monty Sunshine (clt), Lonnie Donegan (bjo), Ken Colyer (tpt), Ron Bowden (dms), Jim Bray (bass) and Chris Barber (tmb)

real thing in the early 1950s, and returned to lead the outstanding Ken Colyer's Jazzmen. A disagreement soon led to trombonist Chris Barber leaving to start his own successful career as a bandleader, supported by trumpeter Pat Halcox and clarinettist Monty Sunshine, not to mention the extraordinary Blues-singing of Ottilie Patterson.

The Trad boom was at its height. Jazz clubs sprang up in London and the provinces, providing audiences for both local and visiting bands. Names suddenly became well known; some remained so, some sank back to obscurity, some moved out of the Trad stream by natural musical evolution, such as Humphrey Lyttelton. Clarinettists were well to the fore: Mister Acker Bilk, with his hit, *Stranger on the Shore*; the late Sandy Brown in duo with trumpeter Al Fairweather; Cy Laurie, an early mystic and cult-figure; Terry Lightfoot, a leader from 1954; Monty Sunshine, his famous hit being *Petite Fleur*. Trumpeters not mentioned above included Alan Elsdon and Alex Welsh, the latter still producing highly-polished Jazz and noteworthy also for turning down an invitation to join Jack Teagarden. And the 1950s also saw the rise of singer George Melly, originally inspired by Bessie Smith and singing with Mick Mulligan's Magnolia Jazz Band, later gigging in the evenings and writing reviews and critiques during the day. He has recently returned with an ever-widening repertoire, touring with Jazz historian and trumpeter John Chilton's Feetwarmers.

These are some of the foremost names of British Trad, many of whom have a wide reputation outside the country; there are hundreds, if not thousands, of other musicians who first took up their instruments at that time, and found them impossible to put down again.

Buck Clayton and Alex Welsh

Cleo Laine and John Dankworth

The late Tubby Hayes, Ronnie Scott, Peter King and Ronnie Ross – four British reedsmen

Ronnie Scott

In 1955, the Musicians' Unions sorted out their difficulties and at long last a procession of American Jazzmen was able to visit the UK, play to the packed houses which eagerly awaited them, and praise many of the home-grown musicians who supported them.

The Trad boom was not the only event in British popular music in the late 1940s and 1950s. In the latter decade, there was the sudden appearance of Skiffle Groups (no less happy, perhaps, but from a totally different culture from that of their begetters, the Spasm Bands of old) inspired by banjo/guitarist Lonnie Donegan who hit on a particular formula and made the most of it.

The film *Rock Around the Clock* with Bill Hailey and his Comets, and Elvis Presley, hit these shores, and there was another highly-copyable formula which became intertwined with Skiffle at the edges and eventually gave rise to the new industry of Pop Music. Whether some of these manifestations were and are a part of the World of Jazz is debatable. In retrospect the movement, although it gave rise to much less-than-mediocre sound, did promote yet another interest in music and performance in general and launch some musicians and entertainers without whom we should be the poorer.

But perhaps that was a sideline. More important to the Jazz scene were the recordings which introduced a new movement called Bop, though one wonders how many of its growing following knew what it was about. Those of the post-war musical generation who were steeped in Trad eschewed Modern Jazz, since they eschewed the saxophone, which seemed to be an essential ingredient of modernism, as being untrue to the roots of the music.

Two men who did take the trouble to find out what was happening were Johnny Dankworth and Ronnie Scott. Reedsmen playing on transatlantic liners, they heard Charlie Parker in New York, came away inspired by

Django Reinhardt (1910–53), Belgian-born guitarist, for many years associated with Stephane Grappelli

Stephane Grappelli

Sidney Bechet (1897–1959), New Orleans clarinettist and soprano sax player – worked with everyone in New Oreleans, Chicago and New York, toured widely from the mid-1920s, and lived his last eight years in Paris

Singer Beryl Bryden here plays washboard with Claude Luter

what he was doing, and translated it into their own terms. Dankworth formed the Johnny Dankworth 7 in 1950, and his first Big Band in 1953, two years after featuring the phenomenal singer Cleo Laine, whom he later married. As well as leading his band, Dankworth has gone on to compose and direct countless film and television scores, one of the UK's most prolific and foremost musicians in the field. Cleo Laine has widened her career from singing Jazz, but her style has no equal anywhere.

Ronnie Scott formed his own band in 1952. Five years later, with another tenorman, the late Tubby Hayes, he founded the Scott–Hayes Jazz Couriers which purveyed Hard Bop for some two-and-a-half years. In 1959 he opened a Jazz Club, now in Frith Street, which has built up a substantial reputation over the years as *the* place where visiting musicians appear in London. He himself continues to play.

In France, the late Hugues Panassié, critic and champion of the Jazz-is-a-Black-Music theory – possibly harmful at the time; certainly amusing in retrospect – founded the Hot Club of France with its famous Quintet in 1934. This comprised the still-swinging violinist Stephane Grappelli, and the Belgian-born guitarist, the late Django Reinhardt, supported by Django's brother Joseph and Roger Chaput on guitars and bassist Louis Vola. The Quintet disbanded in 1939 when Grappelli came to England; he continues to tour widely and play delightfully.

In France, as in England, the development of Jazz after the war followed Trad and Modern streams. Dixieland Bands were led by the clarinettists Claude Luter and Maxim Saury. The country was also the second home of many American musicians, among them Sidney Bechet, Kenny Clarke, Bill Coleman, Mezz Mezzrow, Albert Nicholas and Bud Powell. Kenny Clarke and the Belgian-born pianist Francy Boland formed the Clarke-Boland Big Band in 1962, which for over a decade offered a cosmopolitan focus for European and other visiting musicians; for example, trumpeters who passed through were the Scottish Jimmy Deuchar, the Yugoslavian Dusko Goykovitch and the German Manfred Schoof, all widely experienced musicians and composers.

A final trio from the diverse musical talent of France is the Ellington-inspired Claude Bolling, leader of a Big Band from the mid-1950s and

Claude Bolling's Steffy Club Gang – Gerard Bayol (cnt), Maxim Saury (clt & sop), Benny Vasseur (tmb), Claude Bolling (pno), Robert Escuras (gtr), Guy de Fatto (bass), Robert Peguet (dms)

Michel Legrand

Peter Brötzmann

Jean-Luc Ponty

Alex von Schlippenbach

Joachim Kuhn

Albert Mangelsdorff

Lars Gullin

composer of much film music; composer and pianist Michel Legrand who, among his many other achievements scored *Lady Sings the Blues*; and Jean-Luc Ponty, originally a Jazz violinist who has lately moved into much wider areas of experiment.

Germany, too, has a flourishing Jazz fraternity. Before the war, the music was frowned upon as decadent; afterward this stifling attitude has been handsomely swept away. Among the best-known musicians are multi-instrumentalists Wolfgang Dauner and Joki Freund, tenorman Hans Koller and trombonist Albert Mangelsdorff. There is trumpeter Uli Beckerhoff, and pianist Horst Jankowski of *A Walk in the Black Forest* fame – a reminder of how the right people can be remembered for the wrong things. Reedsmen Peter Brötzmann and Klaus Doldinger started as Dixieland musicians and moved to the other end of the spectrum; pianists Friedrich Gulda and Joachim Kuhn started outside the world of Jazz and moved into it. Another pianist, Alexander von Schlippenbach, is one of the foremost European exponents of Free Jazz.

In countries behind the Iron Curtain Jazz flourishes, despite at one time being frowned on culturally. Some musicians have stayed, others have moved to the West. Festivals, cultural exchanges and broadcast performances have all flourished during the last two decades: Jazz has acquired respectability.

There is a widespread interest in the music – especially Modern Jazz – in Scandinavia: Denmark, Finland, Norway and especially Sweden. Names foremost in Scandinavia, and far beyond, are led by the late Lars Gullin, baritone saxophonist inspired by Gerry Mulligan. Other reedsmen include Hacke Bjorksten, Arne Domnerus, Bjarne Nerem and Eero Koivistoinen.

Jazz in the USSR – March 1978 jam session at Kvadrat Jazz Club, Leningrad, to celebrate the 20th anniversary of the Leningrad Dixieland Jazz Band

There are trumpeters Jan Allen and Bengt-Arne Wallin – now a composer of some note; trombonists Aake Persson and Eje Thelin; pianists Bengt Hallberg, Nils Lindberg and Lars Sjosten; Czechoslovakian-born bassist Georg Riedel; and drummer Edward Vesala. Scandinavian emigrés to the US have included two outstanding Danish-born musicians: bassist Oersted Pedersen and trombonist Kai Winding.

Perhaps the most astonishing rise in Jazz-consciousness in recent years has been seen in Japan. However much a country may wish to Westernize itself, any change in its artistic heritage and outlook has to come from within, and somehow it has. The veteran trumpeter Fumio Nanri was dubbed 'Satchmo of Japan' by Louis Armstrong himself. The Manchurian-born pianist, composer and teacher, Toshiko Akiyoshi, has been dividing her time between the US and Japan since 1956, at which time her quartet was taken over by reedsman Sadao Watanabe. Pianists Mikio Masuda and Masahiko Sato

Bengt Hallberg – Sweden

Oersted Pedersen – Denmark

William Breuker – Holland

Dudu Puckwana – South Africa

Louis Moholo – South Africa

Mongezi Feza (tpt) and Harvey Miller (bass) – SA

Sadao Watanabe – Japan

have also commuted between the US and Japan, as has guitarist Yoshiaki Masuo. Drummer George Otsuka, after playing with reedsmen Watanabe and Sleepy Matsumoto branched out to form his own group. Reedsman Toshiyuki Miyama has been leading his own band since 1950; first the ten-piece Jive Aces, then his New Herd Orchestra of some twenty musicians. The American influence is obvious.

In this lightning tour of the world, we have peeped at a few of the more important countries in the world of Jazz, and mentioned a very small fraction of the musicians therein. We have, however, shown that there is absolutely no doubt that Jazz, in all its various forms, is a worldwide language. Whereas at one time the best that could be hoped for was a second-hand copy of someone else's music, nowadays all nations contribute, and everyone learns from everyone else. I repeat the first sentence of the chapter: Jazz is now a truly international music.

Lew Tabackin (tenor & flute) and Toshiko Akiyoshi – Japan

Yoshaki Masuo – Japan

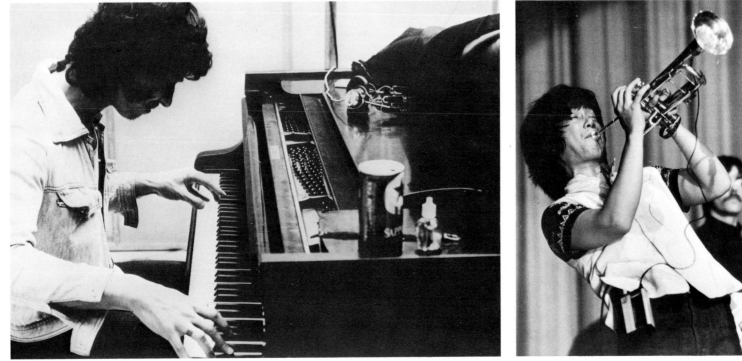

Mikio Masuda – Japan

Tiger Okoshi – Japan

APPENDIX I: SIMPLE JAZZ CHORDS

Although this section is not essential reading, it may prove helpful in understanding the characters of, and differences between, the basic styles of music discussed in this book.

If you are able to play a musical instrument, but know little of chords, this exposition may give you a different outlook on music. Even if you can't play an instrument, you may find some insight here into the way tunes are put together. If possible, experiment with the chords shown in the following diagrams on a keyboard instrument such as a piano.

Look at Fig. 1 and observe the pattern of the keys. The white notes are lettered from A to G, a sequence which repeats from the lower, left-hand end of the keyboard right up to the top, right-hand end. The black notes are grouped in twos and threes, and

each has two names; either the *sharp* (#) of the white note below it, or the *flat* (♭) of the white above it.

If we choose any particular note, and play up or down the keyboard, we find that there are six white and five black keys before we return to another with the same letter as that from which we started. The *interval* between our starting and finishing notes is called an *octave*. The interval between two adjacent notes is a *semitone*.

Now start on a C and play all the white notes, one after the other, up to the next C: C, D, E, F, G, A, B, C. This is a *diatonic scale* in the key of C major, and will be familiar in sound, if not in practice, to most readers. The major scale in C is the only one which can be played wholly on white notes.

Fig. 2 shows the names of the intervals in the C scale. Intervals are the distances between notes, so that any two notes on the keyboard 7 semitones apart constitute a fifth: not just C and G, but C# and G#, D and A, and so on.

Fig. 3 shows a *common chord* in the key of

C: C, E, G and C. Combinations of Cs, Es and Gs up and down the keyboard give *inversions* of the common chord. If you have the opportunity for experiment, you will find that some sound better and fuller than others.

Experiment will also show that diatonic scales can be played starting on any note. F and G scales each need one black note: F uses B♭ and G uses F# as shown in Fig. 4. Similarly, we can find our common chords in F and G: F, A, C, F and G, B, D, G respectively, as in Fig. 5.

Figure 2

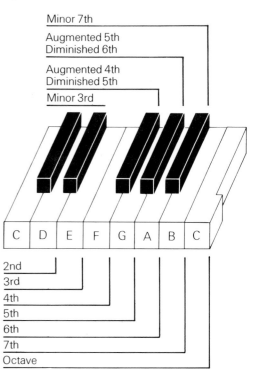

Figure 1

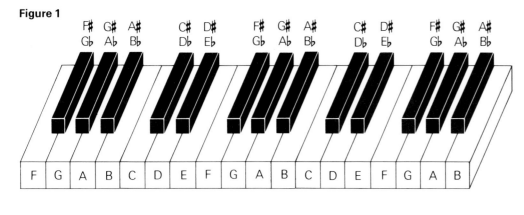

Figure 3

Figure 4

Figure 5

There are eleven diatonic scales according to the note on which we start: Bb and its common chord are shown in Fig. 6, D and its common chord in Fig. 7. To elaborate further would be superfluous if you have a keyboard, and tedious if you have not. We will therefore move on to build up a *chord sequence* from what we have learned so far.

Before that, however, we need one more ingredient: a method of indicating rhythm. Music is broken into pieces of regular length called *bars* and we indicate these by boxes, each of which must be thought of as containing four *beats*, as shown in Fig. 8: 4 bars each of 4 beats of C.

We will now use C, F and G to stand for the common chords in those keys. Fig. 9 shows an 8-bar sequence: play the common chord shown on the first beat of the bar, counting 1, 2, 3, 4; 1, 2, 3, 4 etc to the end. This is a rudimentary accompaniment to a simple, well-known tune – *Little Brown Jug* – in the key of C.

It can of course be played in any key, and Fig. 10 shows it *transposed* into the key of F.

If we are to improve our range of music, we need something more ambitious than the common chords.

The next most useful chords are the *sevenths* (properly, minor sevenths), which add the note one tone below the octave and contribute an expectant quality to the common chord. C[7], F[7], and G[7] are shown in Figs. 11–13; when played, C[7] expects, or resolves to, F; similarly G[7] resolves to C.

Finally, Figs. 14–16 give a selection of other chords, which can of course be transposed into any key, though an ability to do so is another matter.

Now that we have some idea of the makings of chord sequences, we can look at one or two. While not necessarily understanding them, we will be able to see some essential differences between the various styles of music we have discussed so far.

Figure 6

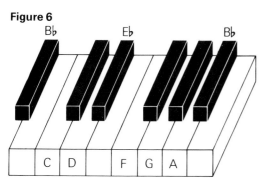

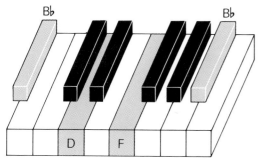

Figure 7

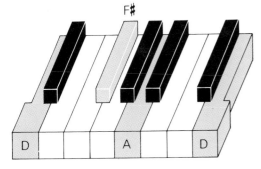

Figure 8

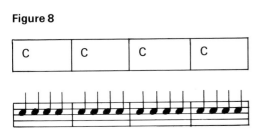

Figure 9

C	F	G	C
C	F	G	C

Figure 10

F	Bb	C	F
F	Bb	C	F

Figure 11

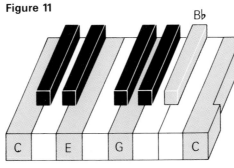

Figure 12

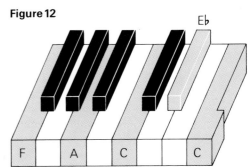

Figure 13

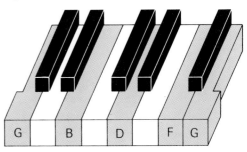

Figure 14
C minor

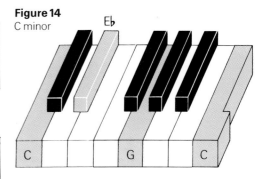

Figure 15
C augmented

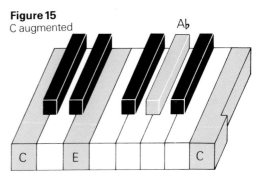

Figure 16
C diminished

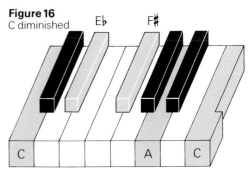

Fig. 17 shows an 8-bar Blues sequence. Fig. 18 shows the way in which the end of that sequence may be modified so that it runs on to another 8, nearly identical, bars, to give a 16-bar sequence; Fig. 19 shows an elaborated version of the 16-bar form.

Fig. 20 shows a 12-bar Blues, and Fig. 21 shows another, developed 12-bar form. However endless the variations which may be performed within these frameworks, the frameworks themselves are rigid.

If we now look at Fig. 22, we find a very different state of affairs. This is a chord sequence for a well-known Jazz standard – rather like *High Society*. Here there is much more than a simple 12-bar sequence, but it is not just that it is longer; it has distinct parts – an introduction or *intro*; a first *strain* leading to a second, which is played twice; a *bridge* leading to a third strain in a different key (containing a *cadenza* or *break* during which a single instrument may perform a solo) which is the main part of the tune; a

fourth strain which may be interposed between playings of the third to add variety and, perhaps, introduce a soloist; and a *coda* or *tag*. This shows the range of sequences in a New Orleans tune which has developed from a march, and shows many of the characteristics of a march. Once again, there is no substitute for listening to performances to hear the differences between the Blues and New Orleans music.

Fig. 23 gives a sequence for a Ragtime piece, which shows many similarities to the march-type tune; how much each owes to the other will again be apparent from playing and listening.

The Blues is not necessarily a more limited musical form just because its framework is tighter than those at which we have just been looking; it is simply different, even though it is represented as using the same essential chords. Until the turn of the century, when they began to merge, New Orleans music and the Blues had travelled

along distinctly different paths.

There is, however, one final point arising out of our discussion. Ragtime, in its piano music, was essentially written in the conventional way, and its performers could read. So also could musicians trained in marching bands, generally speaking; that is the only way of co-ordinating a large group. The emergence of Jazz as an improvised form gave rise to non-reading musicians, and by extension to the idea that Jazz musicians could not read music. (The fact that notation of the rhythmic nuances of Jazz is very difficult is by the way.) But as the chapter on Big Bands has shown, it was not long before reading musicians returned to the world of Jazz for various reasons.

Figure 17

F	F7	Bb	./.
F	C	F	./.

Figure 18

F	F7	Bb	./.
F	C	F	C
F	F7	Bb	./.
F	C	F	./.

Figure 19

F	C7	F	Bb
F	C7	F	C7 C+
F	F7	Bb	Fo
F	C7	F Bb	C7 C+

Figure 20

F	./.	./.	F7
Bb	./.	F	./.
C	./.	F	./.

Figure 21

F F7	Bb Bbm	F C7	F F7
Bb	Fo	F	D
G G7	C C7	F Bb	C7 C+

Figure 22

Introduction

Bb	F	./.	F7

First strain

F	F7	Bb	./.
F7	./.	Bb	./.
Gm	./.	D7	Gm
Gm	./.	C7	F7

Second strain

F7	./.	Bb	./.
C7	./.	F7	./.
Bb	Bb7	Eb	Ebm
Bb	F7	Bb	./. :

Bridge

Bb7	Ebo	Bb7 Ebo	Bb7

Third strain

Eb	./.	./.	./.
./.	Eb Ab	Eb	./.
Bb7	./.	Eb	./.
F7	./.	Break	
Eb	./.	./.	./.
./.	Eb Ab	Eb	Eb7
Ab	Abm	Eb	C7
F7	Bb7	Eb	./.

Fourth strain

Cm	./.	G7	./.
Cm	Cm Fo	G7	./.
Ab	Fm	Eb	Cm
F7	./.	Bb7	./.

Coda

Ab	Abm	Eb	C7
F7	Bb7	Eb	./.
Ab Abm	Bb Eb		

Figure 23

First strain

Bb Bb7	Eb Ebm	Bb	F7	Bb
Bb Bb7	Eb		C7	F7
Bb Bb7	Eb Ebm	Bb	F7	Bb
Bb Bb7	Eb Ebm	Bb	F7	Bb :

Second strain

Bb	./.	Eb Ebm	Bb
B	./.	C7	F7
Bb	./.	Eb Ebm	Bb
Eb Ebm	Bb G	C7 F7	Bb :

Third strain

Eb	Ab	Cm	Fm
Fm	Eb Cm	D7	Gm Bb7
Eb	Ab	Cm	Fm
Fm	Eb C7	F7 Bb7	Eb

Bridge

Eb Ebm	Bb	C F	Bb

Fourth strain

Cm	Eb	Bb	./.
F	./.	F#	Bb
Cm	Eb	Bb	./.
Eb Ebm	Bb	C7 F7	Bb :

APPENDIX 2: TECHNOLOGY AND JAZZ

The role of the phonograph in bringing Jazz to a wider public, and the influence of technological development on the art form deserves a separate assessment here.

THE PHONOGRAPH

The Edison Speaking Machine came on to the market about a century ago and, at about the time that Jazz was coming into being, the phonograph was a novelty that had found its way into many homes. But the early phonograph had one major disadvantage: the recording artists had to perform into large horns to concentrate the sound on to the diaphragm which activated the cutting stylus, and this produced recordings of very low quality by present-day standards, with tiresome resonances and a great deal of high frequency noise. And so, by the time that the first Jazz recording was made (by the ODJB in 1917), the novelty interest of the phonograph had been replaced by frustration that its quality of reproduction could not be improved.

The method of acoustic recording was such that it thrived on strident sounds – instruments with a sharp attack came over very well. The ODJB was able to provide such strident sounds in the course of duty, encouraged no doubt both by a desire to overcome some of the disadvantages of the medium and by the need to provide what they believed their public expected from a Jazz band. Amongst other early recordings, they made *Livery Stable Blues/The Dixie Jazz Band One Step*, released in the US in 1917; and *Barnyard Blues/At The Jazz Band Ball*, released in the UK in 1919. These releases helped both to spread Jazz and to confirm the opinion of the stuffy, older generation that Jazz was simply a degenerate, worthless noise: the kind of reaction which has frequently greeted progress in the arts.

Apart from helping to spread the sound of Jazz for good or ill, recording did many other things. It favored those instruments which were more recordable; it even modified techniques, for example when the drummer introduced wood blocks, skulls and cow bells to give distinctive audible sounds, since the low frequencies of the bass drum were lost and the high frequencies of the cymbals were indistinguishable from the hiss; and it set down for posterity what the early performers actually sounded like. Recording on 78s, with their $3\frac{1}{2}$-minute constraint, was of course a good discipline, which gave a tight, no-nonsense, rounded quality to early recorded music; and because we are conditioned to think of the numbers on, or transcribed from, 78s as though they were typical of the period, the music seems to contrast very favorably with the frequently more rambling style adopted since the advent of the LP.

Electrical recording started to come into its own by the mid-1920s; with this technological advance, recording quality improved considerably, and the effect was as marked on Jazz as on any other sound. However, as always, we find a counter-effect: those who recorded are remembered, those who did not are forgotten. Bands of musicians who assembled for one or two recording dates have become fixed in the mind as permanencies, whereas they were often the most transient. Weighing the evidence, however, there is no doubt that recording has had a beneficial effect on the spread, understanding and appreciation of Jazz, as well as providing a rich source for the musical historian, and for the emerging musician to copy.

Acoustic recording studio 1925

PIANO ROLLS

As far as the piano-roll was concerned, although the technique of manufacture was established in time to capture some early performers, it should not be regarded with too much awe. By the 1920s the equipment had become as good as it was going to be; the recording piano determined the tempo and rubato of the performer, and volume was coded afterward by an editor, and approved by the pianist – giving rise to such comments as: 'That's how I'd like to have played it.' Only a handful of studios used these advanced techniques, however, and Jazz piano-rolls rely on the pedaller to control the expression. As an accurate account of the original performance, piano-rolls must be regarded with some suspicion (mistakes sometimes crept in when they were copied in quantity), and those transcribed on to disc owe as much to the operator as the performer.

RADIO AND TELEVISION

At about the same time as electrical recording came into its own, radio broadcasting began its public career. Although it did little for Jazz in its early days, it gradually came to do its share in promulgating the music though, as always, the prejudices of program controllers had a lot to do with what was and what was not performed, and under which title it was classified.

Television too, with the same reservations, has been of enormous value in bringing Jazz to a wider audience, with the added attraction that the personalities of the musicians come across as they talk about and play the music – even allowing for the amount of time devoted to close-ups of hands.

THE MOVIES

Outside the home, movies brought Jazz and other popular music to the public. The first, and highly successful, talking picture was *The Jazz Singer* (1927) which, allowing for the misleading title, at least made people say the word.

Pennies from Heaven, featuring Louis Armstrong and Bing Crosby, appeared in 1936, and from then on the medium was as important in turning musicians into entertainers as it was in spreading the sound of Jazz. It also encouraged composers to write film music (good), and movie makers to produce spurious biographical accounts of Jazz musicians (bad).

Both film and television have encouraged the making of documentaries (often very good) about musical events.

ELECTRONICS

The development of what we now call electronics for the media discussed above had an effect on bands outside the studios. At first, microphones, amplifiers and speakers were set up in the band to enhance the sounds of quieter instruments, including the human voice which soon was unable to do without such artificial aids. Then every instrument had to have its microphone; problems of balance arose; the volume became louder and louder. The louder it became, the louder people wanted it, until ears became permanently damaged.

The development in the mid-1950s, of the transistor amplifier, able to handle the very sharp attack of the guitar, had an obvious and lasting effect on the pop music world. Nowadays, there is so much artificiality that the sounds we hear owe a disproportionate debt to the producers and technicians.

The latest electronics aids to music-making 1979

DIRECTORY OF MUSICIANS

The following list of jazz musicians gives details of their musical specialities, the names of other musicians or types of music with which each is particularly associated, given in brackets, and, where appropriate, titles of biographies and autobiographies (the author's name is omitted if the latter).

Henry 'Red' Allen: trumpet, singer (Louis Armstrong, Sidney Bechet, Lionel Hampton, Coleman Hawkins, Fletcher Henderson, Billie Holiday, Spike Hughes, James P. Johnson, Jelly Roll Morton, King Oliver, Luis Russell).
Albert Ammons: piano (Boogie Woogie).
Ivie Anderson: singer (Duke Ellington).
Louis Armstrong, 'Satchmo' (Daniel Louis Armstrong): cornet, singer, trumpet, leader (King Oliver, Ma Rainey, Bessie Smith).
  Horn of plenty (Robert Goffin).
  Louis (Max Jones and John Chilton).
  Louis Armstrong (Richard Merryman).
  Louis Armstrong (Hugues Panassié).
  Louis Armstrong (Kenneth G. Richards).
  Satchmo: my life in New Orleans.

Mildred Bailey (née Rinker): singer (Dorsey Brothers, Paul Whiteman).
Paul Barbarin: drums (Henry Red Allen, Louis Armstrong, King Oliver, Luis Russell).
Charlie Barnet (Charles Daly Barnet): alto sax, soprano sax, tenor sax, leader (Benny Carter).
Count Basie (William Basie): organ, piano, composer/arranger, leader (Charlie Christian, Lester Young).
  Count Basie and his orchestra (Raymond Horricks).
Sidney Bechet: clarinet, soprano sax (Louis Armstrong, Eddie Condon, Jelly Roll Morton, Clarence Williams).
  Treat it gentle
Bix Beiderbecke (Leon Bismarck Beiderbecke): clarinet, piano, composer/arranger (Paul Whiteman).
  Bix, man and legend (Richard M. Sudhalter and Philip R. Evans).
  Remembering Bix (Ralph Barton).
Barney Bigard (Leon Albany Bigard): clarinet (Louis Armstrong, Duke Ellington, Art Hodes, Jelly Roll Morton, King Oliver, Luis Russell).
Art Blakey: drums, leader (Jazz Messengers, Thelonious Monk, Horace Silver).
Ruby Braff (Reuben Braff): trumpet (Vic Dickenson, Bud Freeman, Mel Powell).
Bob Brookmeyer (Robert Brookmeyer): piano, valve trombone, composer/arranger (Stan Getz, Gerry Mulligan, Clark Terry).
Big Bill Broonzy (William Lee Conley Broonzy): guitar, singer (Washboard Sam, Sonny Boy Williamson).
  Big Bill Blues (Yannick Bruynoghl).
Sandy Brown (Alexander Brown): clarinet (Sammy Price).
Dave Brubeck (David W. Brubeck): piano, composer/arranger (Paul Desmond).
Georg Brunis (George Brunies): trombone (Eddie Condon, New Orleans Rhythm Kings, Muggsy Spanier).

Harry Carney (Harry Howell Carney): baritone sax (Benny Carter, Duke Ellington, Lionel Hampton, Johnny Hodges, Billie Holiday, Teddy Wilson).
Benny Carter (Bennett Lester Carter): alto sax, clarinet, tenor sax, composer/arranger (Count Basie, Lionel Hampton, Coleman Hawkins, Fletcher Henderson, Billie Holiday, Spike Hughes, McKinney's Cotton Pickers, Ethel Waters).
Big Sid Catlett (Sidney Catlett): drums (Henry Red Allen, Louis Armstrong, Sidney Bechet, Benny Carter, Bud Freeman, Dizzy Gillespie, Benny Goodman, Coleman Hawkins, Fletcher Henderson, Spike Hughes, Don Redman).
Ray Charles: piano, singer, composer/arranger
George Chisholm: trombone (Benny Carter, Wild Bill Davison, Alex Welsh).
Buck Clayton (Wilbur Clayton): trumpet, composer/arranger (Count Basie, Billie Holiday, Jimmy Rushing, Buddy Tate, Lester Young).
Nat King Cole (Nathaniel Coles): piano, singer (Lester Young).
  Nat King Cole (Maria Cole and Louie Robinson).
Cozy Cole (William Randolph Cole): drums (Louis Armstrong, Cab Calloway, Dizzy Gillespie, Lionel Hampton, Coleman Hawkins, Earl Hines, Jelly Roll Morton, Stuff Smith).
Bill Coleman (William Johnson Coleman): trumpet (Luis Russell, Lester Young).
Ornette Coleman: alto sax, composer/arranger.
John Coltrane (John William Coltrane): tenor sax (Don Cherry, Miles Davis, Thelonious Monk).
  Coltrane: a biography (C. O. Simpkins).
Eddie Condon (Albert Edwin Condon): banjo, guitar, leader (Louis Armstrong, Bud Freeman, Jack Teagarden).
  We called it music (Eddie Condon and Thomas Sugrue).
Ida Cox: singer (King Oliver).
Bob Crosby (George Robert Crosby): singer, leader (Dorsey Brothers).

Tadd Dameron (Tadley Ewing Dameron): piano, composer/arranger (Billy Eckstine, Dizzy Gillespie, Fats Navarro).
John Dankworth (John Philip William Dankworth): clarinet, alto sax, composer/arranger.
Eddie 'Lockjaw' Davis: tenor sax (Count Basie).
Miles Davis (Miles Dewey Davis): flügelhorn, trumpet.
  Miles Davis (Bill Cole).
Wild Bill Davison (William Edward Davison): clarinet, trumpet, leader (Sidney Bechet, Eddie Condon, Tony Parenti).
Buddy de Franco (Boniface Ferdinand Leonardo de Franco): bass clarinet, clarinet, composer/arranger (Sidney Bechet, Sidney and Wilbur de Paris, McKinney's Cotton Pickers, Jelly Roll Morton, Don Redman).
Vic Dickenson (Victor Dickenson): singer, trombone, composer/arranger (Sidney Bechet, Ruby Braff, Benny Carter, Buck Clayton, Bobby Hackett, Billie Holiday, Buddy Tate, Lester Young).
Baby Dodds (Warren Dodds): drums (Louis Armstrong, Johnny Dodds, Bunk Johnson, George Lewis, Jelly Roll Morton, Albert Nicholas, King Oliver).
Johnny Dodds: clarinet (Louis Armstrong, Lovie Austin's Blues Serenaders, Ida Cox, Jelly Roll Morton, King Oliver).
Natty Dominique (Anatie Dominique): trumpet (Johnny Dodds, Jelly Roll Morton, Jimmie Noone).
Jimmy Dorsey (James Dorsey): alto sax, clarinet, leader (Dorsey Brothers, Benny Goodman, Coleman Hawkins, Miff Mole, Red Nichols, Jack Teagarden, Joe Venuti).
Tommy Dorsey (Thomas Dorsey): trombone, leader (Dorsey Brothers, Benny Goodman, Joe Venuti, Paul Whiteman).
  Tommy and Jimmy: the Dorsey years (Herb Sanford).

Harry 'Sweets' Edison: trumpet (Count Basie, Louis Bellson, Duke Ellington, Ella Fitzgerald, Barney Kessel, Red Norvo, Art Tatum, Jimmy Witherspoon).
Roy Eldridge (David Roy Eldridge): drums, flügelhorn, singer, trumpet (Count Basie, Bud Freeman, Dizzy Gillespie, Benny Goodman, Coleman Hawkins, Fletcher Henderson, Johnny Hodges, Billie Holiday, Gene Krupa, Artie Shaw, Buddy Tate, Art Tatum, Joe Turner, Ben Webster, Teddy Wilson, Lester Young).
Duke Ellington (Edward Kennedy Ellington): piano, composer/arranger, leader
  Duke Ellington (Barry Ulanov).
  Music is my mistress.
  The world of Duke Ellington (Stanley Dance).
Gil Evans (Ian Ernest Gilmore Green): piano, composer/arranger (Miles Davis).

Maynard Ferguson: trumpet, valve trombone, leader (Stan Kenton, Shorty Rogers).
Ella Fitzgerald: singer
Bud Freeman (Lawrence Freeman): tenor sax (Louis Armstrong, Eddie Condon, Dorsey Brothers, Benny Goodman, Mezz Mezzrow, Jack Teagarden, Bob Wilber, Lee Wiley).
  You don't look like a musician

Erroll Garner: piano, composer/arranger (Charlie Parker).
Stan Getz (Stanley Getz): tenor sax (Woody Herman).
Dizzy Gillespie (John Birks Gillespie): singer, trumpet, composer/arranger, leader (Charlie Christian, Stan Getz, Charlie Parker, Oscar Peterson).
Benny Goodman (Benjamin David Goodman): clarinet, leader (Charlie Christian, Billie Holiday, Ben Pollack, Adrian Rollini, Joe Venuti, Lester Young).
  BG off the record
  BG on the record (D. Russell Connor and Warren W. Hicks).
  The kingdom of swing (Benny Goodman and Irving Kolodin).
Stephane Grappelli: violin (Jean-Luc Ponty, Django Reinhardt).

Bobby Hackett (Robert Leo Hackett): clarinet, guitar, trumpet (Eddie Condon, Benny Goodman, Miff Mole, Jack Teagarden).
Edmond Hall: clarinet (Henry Red Allen, Eddie Condon, Sidney de Paris, Vic Dickenson, Claude Hopkins).
Lionel Hampton: drums, piano, vibes, leader (Louis Armstrong, Charlie Christian, Benny Goodman, Art Tatum).
W. C. Handy (William Charles Handy): clarinet, composer/arranger, leader.
  Father of the blues.
Bill Harris (Willard Palmer Harris): trombone (Ralph Burns, Terry Gibbs, Woody Herman, Gene Krupa, Charlie Ventura).
Coleman Hawkins, Bean: tenor sax (Henry Red Allen, Benny Carter, Lionel Hampton, Fletcher Henderson, Spike Hughes, Thelonious Monk, Ma Rainey, Django Reinhardt, Sonny Rollins, Bessie Smith).
Fletcher Henderson, Smack (James Fletcher Henderson): piano, composer/arranger, leader (Benny Goodman, Ma Rainey, Bessie Smith, Trixie Smith, Rex Stewart, Ethel Waters).
  Hendersonia (Walter C. Allen).
Woody Herman (Woodrow Charles Herman): alto sax, clarinet, singer, leader
Earl 'Fatha' Hines (Earl Kenneth Hines): piano, composer/arranger, leader (Louis Armstrong, Jimmie Noone).
Art Hodes (Arthur W. Hodes): piano
Johnny Hodges, Rabbit (John Cornelius Hodges): alto sax (Duke Ellington, Earl Hines, Billie Holiday, Gerry Mulligan, Billy Strayhorn, Teddy Wilson).
Billie Holiday, Lady Day (Eleanor Gough McKay): singer (Artie Shaw, Teddy Wilson, Lester Young).
  Billie's blues (John Chilton).
  Lady sings the blues (Billie Holiday and William Duffy).

Illinois Jacquet (Battiste Illinois Jacquet): tenor sax (Nat King Cole, Dizzy Gillespie, Lester Young).
Harry James (Harry Hagg James): trumpet, leader (Benny Goodman).
Bunk Johnson (William Geary Johnson): cornet, trumpet, leader (Sidney Bechet).
J. J. Johnson (James Louis Johnson): trombone, composer/arranger (Miles Davis, Stan Getz, Sonny Rollins, Sonny Stitt).
James P. Johnson (James Price Johnson): piano, composer/arranger (Eddie Condon, Edmond Hall, Bessie Smith, Jack Teagarden).
Lonnie Johnson (Alonzo Johnson): guitar, singer (Louis Armstrong, Duke Ellington, Eddie Lang).
Pete Johnson: piano (Boogie Woogie, Jimmy Rushing, Joe Turner).
  The Pete Johnson story (Hans J. Maurerer).
Scott Joplin: piano, composer/arranger (Keith Nichols, piano rolls, Joshua Rifkin).
  Scott Joplin and the ragtime era (Peter Gammond).

Stan Kenton (Stanley Newcomb Kenton): piano, composer/arranger, leader
Gene Krupa: drums, leader (Eddie Condon, Benny Goodman, Red Nichols).

Tommy Ladnier (Thomas Ladnier): trumpet (Lovie Austin's Blues Serenaders, Sidney Bechet, Ida Cox, Fletcher Henderson, Ma Rainey, Bessie Smith).
Cleo Laine (née Clementina Dinah Campbell): singer (John Dankworth).
Eddie Lang (Salvatore Massaro): guitar (Bix Beiderbecke, Dorsey Brothers, Red Nichols, Joe Venuti).
Leadbelly (Huddie Ledbetter): guitar, singer
  The Leadbelly songbook (Moses Asch and Alan Lomax).
Peggy Lee (née Norma Dolores Egstrom): singer
George Lewis: clarinet (Bunk Johnson).
Meade 'Lux' Lewis: piano (Boogie Woogie).
Jimmie Lunceford (James Melvin Lunceford): leader
Humphrey Lyttelton: trumpet, composer/arranger, leader.

I play as I please
Second chorus
Take it from the top

Wingy Manone (Joseph Manone):
trumpet, singer, leader.
Trumpet on the wing (Wingy Manone and
Paul Vandervoort II).
George Melly: singer (John Chilton, Mick
Mulligan).
Owning up
Rum, Bum and Concertina
Charles Mingus: string bass, piano,
composer/arranger, leader.
Beneath the underdog.
Glenn Miller: trombone, composer/
arranger, leader.
Glen Miller and his orchestra (George T.
Simon).
Moonlight serenade (John Flower).
Thelonious Monk (Thelonious Sphere
Monk): piano, composer/arranger (Art
Blakey).
Jelly Roll Morton (Ferdinand Joseph La
Menthe): piano, composer/arranger (Louis
Armstrong, New Orleans Rhythm Kings).
Mister Jelly Roll (Alan Lomax).
Gerry Mulligan (Gerald Joseph
Mulligan): baritone sax, piano, composer/
arranger (Miles Davis).

Ray Nance (Willis Nance): singer,
trumpet, violin (Duke Ellington, Earl
Hines, Johnny Hodges, Shelly Manne).
Joseph 'Tricky Sam' Nanton: trombone
(Duke Ellington).
Fats Navarro (Theodore Navarro):
trumpet (Tadd Dameron, Billy Eckstine,
Charlie Parker).
Albert Nicholas: clarinet (Sidney Bechet,
Jelly Roll Morton, King Oliver, Adrian
Rollini, Luis Russell).
Red Nichols (Ernest Loring Nichols):
cornet, leader (Benny Goodman, Jack
Teagarden).
The five pennies (Grady Johnson).
Jimmie Noone: clarinet, leader (Louis
Armstrong, Johnny Dodds, Earl Hines,
King Oliver).
Red Norvo (Kenneth Norville): vibes,
xylophone, leader (Mildred Bailey, Benny
Goodman, Woody Herman, Gerry
Mulligan).

King Oliver (Joseph Oliver): cornet,
leader (Louis Armstrong).
King Joe Oliver (Walter C. Allen and
Brian A. L. Rust).
Kid Ory (Edward Ory): trombone,
composer/arranger, leader (Louis

Armstrong, Johnny Dodds, Jelly Roll
Morton, King Oliver).

Charlie Parker, Bird (Charles Christopher
Parker Jr): alto sax, composer/arranger
(Miles Davis, Dizzy Gillespie, Jay
McShann).
Bird lives (Ross Russell).
Charlie Parker (Max Harrison).
The legend of Charlie Parker (Robert G.
Reisner).
Oscar Peterson (Oscar Emmanuel
Peterson): piano, singer, composer/arranger
(Charlie Parker, Sonny Stitt, Ben Webster).
Earl 'Bud' Powell: piano, composer/
arranger (Dexter Gordon, Coleman
Hawkins, Charlie Parker).
Sammy Price (Samuel Blythe Price):
piano, leader (Henry Red Allen, Sidney
Bechet, Mezz Mezzrow, Jimmy Rushing).
Russell Procope: alto sax, clarinet,
soprano sax (Duke Ellington, Coleman
Hawkins, Fletcher Henderson, Earl Hines,
Jelly Roll Morton, Billy Strayhorn,
Clarence Williams).

Ma Rainey (née Gertrude Malissa Nix
Pridgett): singer.
Don Redman (Donald Matthew Redman):
sax, composer/arranger, leader (Louis
Armstrong, Fletcher Henderson,
McKinney's Cotton Pickers, Bessie Smith).
Buddy Rich (Bernard Rich): drums,
singer (Charlie Parker).
Super drummer (Whitney Balliott).
Max Roach (Maxwell Roach): drums
(Clifford Brown, Charlie Parker, Sonny
Rollins).
Adrian Rollini: bass sax, vibes (Bix
Beiderbecke, Benny Goodman, Coleman
Hawkins, Miff Mole, Red Nichols, Joe
Venuti).
Sonny Rollins (Theodore Walter Rollins):
tenor sax (Miles Davis, Thelonious Monk,
Bud Powell).
Jimmy Rushing, Mr Five by Five
(James Andrew Rushing): singer (Count
Basie, Bennie Moten).
Luis Russell (Luis Carl Russell): piano,
composer/arranger, leader (Henry Red
Allen, Louis Armstrong, King Oliver).
Pee Wee Russell (Charles Ellsworth
Russell): clarinet (Bix Beiderbecke, Billy
Banks, Eddie Condon, Bud Freeman,
Coleman Hawkins, Red Nichols, Jack
Teagarden, Teddy Wilson).

Eddie Sauter (Edward Ernest Sauter):
composer/arranger, leader (Mildred Bailey,
Benny Goodman, Peggy Lee, Artie Shaw).

Charlie Shavers (Charles James Shavers):
trumpet, composer/arranger (Sidney
Bechet, Tommy Dorsey, Coleman Hawkins,
Billie Holiday, John Kirby, Jimmie Noone,
Charlie Parker).
Artie Shaw (Arthur Arshawsky): clarinet,
composer/arranger, leader (Bunny Berigan,
Billie Holiday).
The trouble with Cinderella
Archie Shepp: sax, composer/arranger,
leader (John Coltrane, Cecil Taylor).
Horace Silver (Horace Ward Martin
Tavares Silver): piano, composer/arranger.
Omer Simeon (Omer Victor Simeon):
alto sax, clarinet (Wilbur de Paris, Earl
Hines, Jimmie Lunceford, Jelly Roll
Morton, King Oliver, Kid Ory, Tiny
Parham, Jabbo Smith, Jimmy Witherspoon).
Zoot Sims (John Haley Sims): alto sax,
clarinet, tenor sax (Count Basie, Woody
Herman, Gerry Mulligan).
Bessie Smith: singer.
Bessie (Chris Albertson).
Somebody's angel child (Carman Moore).
Joe Smith: trumpet (Fletcher Henderson,
McKinney's Cotton Pickers, Ma Rainey,
Bessie Smith, Ethel Waters).
Stuff Smith (Hezekiah Leroy Gordon
Smith): singer, violin, leader (Dizzy
Gillespie).
Willie 'The Lion' Smith (William Henry
Joseph Berthol Bonaparte Bertholoff Smith):
piano, composer/arranger.
Music on my mind (Willie Smith and
George Hoefer).
Muggsy Spanier (Francis Joseph Spanier):
cornet, leader (Sidney Bechet, Bix
Beiderbecke, New Orleans Rhythm Kings).
Jess Stacey (Jess Alexandria Stacey):
piano (Eddie Condon, Bob Crosby, Benny
Goodman, Lionel Hampton, Harry James).
Rex Stewart (Rex William Stewart):
cornet, trumpet (Duke Ellington, Fletcher
Henderson, Django Reinhardt, Luis
Russell).
Sonny Stitt (Edward Stitt): sax (Dizzy
Gillespie).
Billy Strayhorn, Swee'pea (William
Strayhorn): piano, composer/arranger
(Duke Ellington, Ella Fitzgerald).
Joe Sullivan (Dennis Patrick Terence
Joseph O'Sullivan): piano, composer/
arranger (Louis Armstrong, Eddie Condon,
Bob Crosby, Coleman Hawkins, Muggsy
Spanier, Jack Teagarden).

Art Tatum (Arthur Tatum): piano
Jack Teagarden (Weldon John
Teagarden): singer, trombone, leader
(Louis Armstrong, Benny Goodman, Bobby

Hackett, Paul Whiteman).
Sonny Terry (Saunders Teddell):
harmonica, singer (Blind Boy Fuller,
Leadbelly, Brownie McGhee).
Frankie Trumbauer, Tram: C melody
sax (Bix Beiderbecke, Eddie Lang, Paul
Whiteman).
Big Joe Turner (Joseph Turner): singer

Sarah Vaughan (Sarah Lois Vaughan):
singer (Dizzy Gillespie, Charlie Parker).
Joe Venuti (Giuseppe Venuti): violin,
leader (Bix Beiderbecke, Benny Goodman,
Eddie Lang, Red McKenzie).

Fats Waller (Thomas Wright Waller):
organ, piano, singer, leader (Louis
Armstrong, Billy Banks, Fletcher Henderson,
James P. Johnson, Jack Teagarden).
Ain't misbehavin' (Ed Kirkeby, Sinclair
Traill and Duncan B. Scheidt).
Dinah Washington (Ruth Jones): singer.
Ethel Waters: singer.
His eye is on the sparrow (Ethel Waters and
Charles Samuels).
Muddy Waters (McKinley Morganfield):
guitar, singer.
Chick Webb (William Webb): drums,
leader
Ben Webster (Benjamin Francis Webster):
tenor sax (Willie Bryant, Benny Carter,
Harry Edison, Duke Ellington, Dizzy
Gillespie, Bill Harris, Coleman Hawkins,
Fletcher Henderson, Billie Holiday, Barney
Kessel, John Lewis, Bennie Moten, Charlie
Parker, Art Tatum, Jack Teagarden, Teddy
Wilson, Jimmy Witherspoon).
Paul Whiteman: leader (Bix Beiderbecke,
Jack Teagarden).
Cootie Williams (Charles Melvin
Williams): trumpet, leader (Benny Carter,
Charlie Christian, Duke Ellington, Benny
Goodman, Lionel Hampton, Johnny
Hodges).
Mary Lou Williams (Mary Elfrieda Will):
piano, composer/arranger (Don Byas, Dizzy
Gillespie, Bobby Hackett, Andy Kirk,
Buddy Tate).
Teddy Wilson (Theodore Wilson): piano,
composer/arranger (Mildred Bailey, Willie
Bryant, Benny Carter, Benny Goodman,
Billie Holiday, Red Norvo, Sarah Vaughan,
Lester Young).
Jimmy Yancey (James Yancey): piano.
Lester Young, Prez (Lester Willis Young):
clarinet, tenor sax, composer/arranger
(Count Basie, Nat King Cole, Coleman
Hawkins, Jimmy Rushing).

ACKNOWLEDGEMENTS

The author and publishers would like to thank the following for permission to reproduce illustrations and for supplying photographs (numbers in italics refer to color illustrations):

Bob Adelman 12; Dennis Austin 178 above right; Beryl Bryden 111, 168, 176 right below; Camera Press 8–9, 93 below left, 121, 176 right above; EMI (Capitol Records) 31, 85 top left; Brian Foskett 12 (inset), 34 left and right, 53, 77, 88–9, 90–1, 97, 100 above centre, above right, and below, 101 above left, centre above, and right, 123 (inset), 130 below, 137 above and below, 142, 160 left, 162, 164–5, 171 left and right, 173; Ronald Grant Collection 94–5; H H Electronic 187; *Jazz Journal* 4–5, 32–3 (and title page), 35 left, 55 (inset), 73, 74–5, 82–3 below, 86–7, 92 right, 96–7, 112–13 (copyright by Universal Pictures, a Division of Universal City Studios, Inc. Courtesy of MCA Publishing, a Division of MCA Inc.), 128–9, 130 above, 148 left, 166, 167, 169, 170, 172–3, 174 above and below left, 177, 178 left above, left centre, bottom left, bottom centre, bottom right, 179, 180 centre left, top right, bottom right, 181 above left, bottom left; Jazz Music Books 20–1, 28–9, 35 above and below right, 36–7, 37, 38 (inset), 38–9, 40–1, 42, 43, 44–5, 55, 56, 57, 58, 59 left and right, 64–5, 66, 67, 68 below and above, 69, 71, 72, 76, 78–9, 80–1, 82 left, 82–3 above, 83 right, 84 left above, below and right, 85 below left, and right, 92 left, 93 above, and right, 104–5, 105 (inset), 108–9, 110 above and below, 115, 116 top, 116–17, 117 above left and right, 120, 121 above and below, 124 left, 124–5, 128, 131 above and below right, 132–3, 134, 135, 138, 139, 140–1, 143, 144–5, 149 centre and right, 152 above and below, 155 right, 161, 168 above, 174, 176 left; Alan Johnson 60–1, 62, 63, 70, 100–1 below, 152; Jak Kilby 178 centre right, 180 centre, centre right, bottom left, bottom centre, 181 above right, bottom right; Mansell Collection 14–15, 17; Photo Files 46–7, 50–1; Frederic Ramsey Jr 48, 49; David Redfern *18* top, centre below and bottom, *19*, *22*, *22–3*, *23*, *98*, *99* above left and right, below, *102–3*, *106–7*, *107*, *114–15*, *118* above and below, *119* above left and right, below, *122* above and below, *123*, *126*, *127* above and below, 131 below left, *146*, *147* left, *150* below, *150–1*, *151* top left and right, *154*, *155* left, 157, *158* above and below, *159* right, 160 right, 170 (inset), 172 (insets), 174 below right; Brian Rust 24, 28 (inset), 186; Valerie Wilmer *18* centre above, *26–7*, *33* top, *103* (inset), *147* right, 148–9, *150* top, 156, 157 (inset), *159* below left, 163.

Record labels reproduced from the Les Zeiger Collection.

The author and publishers have taken all possible care to trace and acknowledge the source of illustrations. If any errors have occurred, the publishers will be happy to correct them in future editions.

INDEX

Akiyoshi, Toshiko, 180, *181*
Allen Jan, 180
Ammons, Albert, 73
Armstrong, Lil Hardin *see* Hardin, Lil
Armstrong, Louis, 31, *31*, *32–3*, *34*, 36, 37, 41, 54, 57, 71, 92, 147, 156, 168
Austin High School Gang, *82–3*, 83
Austin, Lovie, 54

Bailey, Mildred, 92, *92*
Baker, Chet, 160
Barber, Chris, *172*, 173
Barnet, Charlie, 128, *129*
Basie, Count, 53, 100, *100*, *102–3*, 110, 152
Beale, Charlie, *32–3*
Bechet, Leonard, 38
Bechet, Sidney, 37, 43, *176*, 177
Beckerhoff, Uli, 179
Beiderbecke, Bix, 79, 83, *84*, *85*, 91, 92
Bell, Graeme, 171
Bigard, Barney, *32–3*, 41, 97, *99*
Bilk, Acker, *139*, *172*, 173
Bjorksten, Hacke, 179
Blakey, Art, 153, 154, *154*, 160, 162
Blues, 48–9, 52–63, 66
Boland, Francy, 177
Bolden, Charles 'Buddy', 17, 18, *20–1*, 138
Bolling, Claude, 177, *177*
Boogie, 71, 73, 136
Bop, 142, 147–50, 152, 153, 154, 156, 159
Breuker, Willem, *180*
Briggs, Pete, 36
Broonzy, 'Big Bill', 59, *59*, 60
Brotzmann, Peter, *178*, 179
Brown, Clifford, 159
Brown, Ray, *19*, 150
Brown, Sandy, 173
Brubeck, Dave, *155*, 155
Brunis, George, 79, *82*
Bryce, Owen, 171

Callendar, Red, *32–3*
Calloway, Cab, 13, 147
Carey, Papa Mutt, 37
Carney, Harry, 97, *99*
Carter, Benny, 168, *168*
Casa Loma Orchestra, 116
Celestin, Papa, 43
Chaput, Roger, 177
Charles, Ray, *137*
Chauvin, Louis, 68
Chilton, John, 173
Chisholm, George, 168
Christian, Charlie, 22, 152, *153*
Christian, Emil, 78
Clarke, Kenny, 148, *148–9*, 149, 150, 159, 177
Clayton, Buck, 53, *118*, 173
Cole, Nat King, 67
Coleman, Bill, *88–9*, 177
Coleman, Ornette, 163, *163*
Coltrane, John, 156, *157*, 158
Colyer, Ken, 171, *171*, 173
Cooper, Andy, *137*
Cornish, Willie, 18
Covington, Warren, 121
Cox, Ida, 54
Crane River Jazz Band, 171, *172–3*

Creath, Charlie, 29

Dameron, Tadd, 154, 155, *155*, 156
Dankworth, John, *174*, 175, 176
Dauner, Wolfgang, 179
Davenport, Cow Cow, 71
Davis, Miles, 18, *18*, 153, 154, 156, 158, *158*, 162
Davis, Peter, 31
Desmond, Paul, 155
Deuchar, Jimmy, 177
Dickerson, Carroll, 34
Dixie music, 76–85
Dixie Syncopators, 43, 76
Doc Cook's Dreamland Orchestra, 43
Doc Malney's Minstrel Show, 25
Dodds, Johnny, 25, *35*, 35–6, 37, 41, 84
Dodds, Warren 'Baby', 35, *35*, 36, 41, 84
Doldinger, Klaus, 179
Dominique, Natty, 35, *35*
Domnerus, Arne, 179
Donegan, Lonnie, 175
Dorsey, Jimmy, 92, 121, *121*
Dorsey, Tommy, 85, 92, 121, *121*
Dreamland Syncopators, 31
Duhé, Lawrence, 41
Dutch Swing College Band, *164–5*, 166, *166*
Dutrey, Honoré, 41

Eckstine, Billy, 147, *147*, 154, 156, 158
Edwards, Eddie, 78
Eldridge, Roy, *119*, 147, 148–9
Elizalde, Fred, 167, *167*
Ellington, Duke, 57, 70, *86–7*, *90*, 91, *96–7*, 97–8, *98*, 100, 110, 114, 168
Ellington, Mercer, 97, 98, 149
Elsdon, Alan, 173
Evans, Gil, 154, 158
Ezell, Will, 30

Fairweather, Al, 173
Fawkes, Wally, 171
Fezi, Mongezi, *180*
Fitzgerald, Ella, 92, *106–7*, 107, 110, 159
Franco, Buddy de, 152, *152*
Freeman, Bud, 77, 82, 83
Freund, Joki, 179

Gershwin, George, 92
Getz, Stan, *159*, 159, 160, 162
Gifford, Gene, 116
Gillespie, Dizzie, *18*, 71, *144–5*, *146*, 147, 148, 149, 150, 152, 154, 155, 156, 158
Goodman, Benny, 22, 43, 73, 82, 85, 93, 110, 114, *116*, 117, *118*, 120–1, 124, 152, 159
Gospel songs, 13
Goykovitch, Dusko, 177
Grantz, Norman, 110
Grappelli, Stephane, 19, *176*, 177
Gray, Glen, 116, *116–17*
Green, Freddie, *101*
Gulda, Friedrich, 179
Gullin, Lars, *178*, 179

Hackett, Bobby, *122*

Halcox, Pat, 77, 173
Hallberg, Bengt, 180, *180*
Hammond, John, 73, 110
Hampton, Lionel, 22, 121, 124, *124*, *126*, 156
Handy, W. C., 63
Hardin, Lil, 31, 36, 41
Harris, Bill, *131*
Hawkins, Coleman, 54, 76, 83, *132–3*, 156
Hayes, Tubby, 176
Heath, Percy, 150
Henderson, Fletcher, 31, 91, 92–3, *93*, 110, 116, 154
Henderson, Horace, 93
Herman, Woody, *18*, 127, 128, *128*, 149, 152, 159
Hilaire, Andrew, *44–5*
Hill, Bertha 'Chippie', 54
Hill, Teddy, 147, 149
Hines, Earl, 34, 43, 70, *70*, 71, 147
Hodges, Johnny, *19*, 97, *97*, 156
Holiday, Billie, 110, *111*
Hot 5, 31, 36, *36–7*, 37, 41
Hot 7, 36, 41
Hughes, Spike, 168

Jackson, Milt, 22, *22*, 151
Jackson, Papa Charlie, 59
Jackson, Quentin, *100*
Jacquet, Illinois, *134*, 156
James, Harry, 82, *127*, 128
Jankowski, Horst, 179
Jazz Messengers, 153, 154, 160
Jefferson, Blind Lemon, *56*, 57, 59
Johnson, Bill, 41
Johnson, Bunk, 41, 138, *138*
Johnson, James P., 54, *69*, 70, 97
Johnson, Jay Jay, 76, 152, *153*
Johnson, Lonnie, 57, *58*
Johnson, Pete, 73, *73*
Jones, Clarence, 34
Joplin, Scott, 67, 68, *68*

Kay, Connie, 150
Kenton, Stan, *114–15*, *131*, 154, 159
Keppard, Freddie, 35, 43
Kessel, Barney, *19*
Kirby, John, *115*
Kirk, Roland, *142*
Koivistoinen, Eero, 179
Koller, Hans, 179
Konitz, Lee, 158
Krupa, Gene, *119*, 121
Kuhn, Joachim, *178*, 179

Ladnier, Tommy, 43, *43*, 54
Laine, Cleo, *174*, 176
Laine, 'Papa Jack', 78, 79
Lang, Eddie, 57, 83, 92
Laurie, Cy, 173
Leadbelly, 22, 57, *57*, 60
Lee, Peggy, 92, *119*
Legrand, Michel, *178*, 179
Lewis, Frank, 18
Lewis, George, 37, 138, *139*
Lewis, John, 150, *151*
Lewis, Meade Lux, 72, 73
Lewis, Ted, 79
Lightfoot, Terry, 173
Lindberg, Nils, 180
Lindsay, John, *44–5*

Lomax, Alan, 43, 57, 60
Lomax, John, 57
Lunceford, Jimmie, *108–9*, 110, 121
Luter, Claude, *176*, 177
Lyttelton, Humphrey, *170*, 171, 173

McGhee, Brownie, 60, *60–1*
McKenzie, Red, 167
McKinney's Cotton Pickers, 93
McPartland, Dick, 83
McPartland, Jimmy, 83, *84*
Mangelsdorff, Albert, *178*, 179
Marable, Fate, 29, 35
Mares, Paul, 79
Masuda, Milio, 180, *181*
Masuo, Yoshiaki, 181, *181*
Matsumoto, Sleepy, 181
Melly, George, 169, *169*, 173
Mezzrow, Mezz, 177
Miles, Lizzie, 54, 57
Miley, Bubber, 97
Milhaud, Darius, 154
Miller, Glen, 82, *120*, 121, *131*, 152
Miller, Harvey, *180*
Millinder, Lucky, 13
Mingus, Charles, 156, *157*
Mitchell, George, *44–5*
Miyama, Toshiyuki, 181
Modern Jazz Quartet, 22, 149, 150, *151*
Moholo, Louis, *180*
Monk, Thelonious, *23*, *143*, 150, *150*
Moore, Oscar, 67
Morton, Jelly Roll, 25, 36, 43, *44–5*, 54, 63, 68, 76, 91, 114
Moten, Benny, 53, 100
Mount City Blue Blowers, 83, 167
Mulligan, Gerry, *18*, 153, 154, 155, 158, 160, *160*

Nance, Ray, 19
Nanri, Fumio, 180
Nanton, Tricky Sam, 97
Navarro, Fats, 156
Nelson, Dave, *50–1*
Nelson, Louis, 138
Nerem, Bjarne, 179
New Orleans, 16, 17, 25, 29
New Orleans Rhythm Kings, 79, *80–1*, 82, 117
New Orleans Seven, *32–3*
Nicholas, Albert, *137*, 177
Nichols, Red, *85*
Noone, Jimmie, 37, *42*, 43, 84
Norvo, Red, 22, 92, *130*

Okoshi, Tiger, *181*
Oliver, Joe 'King', 18, 31, 35, 36, 37, 41, 42, 54, 76
Oliver, Sy, 110
Orange Blossom Band, 116
Original Dixieland Jazz Band, 76, 78, *78–9*, 79, 134
Ory, Edward 'Kid', 25, 31, *32–3*, 35, 36, 37, *38–9*, *40–1*, 41, 43, *44–5*, 76, 138, 156
Otsuka, George, 181

Page, Walter, 53
Panassié, Hughes, 177
Parker, Charlie, 71, *144–5*, 148, *148*, 156, 158, 175